"Funny, raw, and packed with truth, this book is offensive in all the right ways...This book reminded me of why I am a Christian, and I wept with gratitude when I finished it."

—Rachel Held Evans, blogger, author of
A Year of Biblical Womanhood

"Nadia has written a wonderful, rule-breaking, stereotype-smashing book that succeeds as a memoir, as a sermon on love, and as a welcome home 'letter' to the rejected. With this book, Nadia will become America's pastor to those alienated from religion but who still crave transcendent purpose and meaning in their lives."

—Frank Schaeffer, author of *Crazy for God*

"Brilliant and hilarious...With this powerful book, Nadia claims the prophetic voice of the apostle to the apostles. And, like Mary Madgdalene, she carries the good news of resurrection to the world."

—Sara Miles, author of *Take This Bread*,
Jesus Freak, and the forthcoming
City of God

"This book is *Mere Christianity* for an altogether new kind of Christianity that's also blessedly ancient. I couldn't turn pages fast enough and yet regretted the book's hastening end."

—Jason Byassee, senior pastor of Boone United
Methodist Church and Fellow in Theology &
Leadership at Duke Divinity School

"Despite her alternative approach, her quirky sermons which are littered with profanities have worked." —*The Daily Mail*

"Bolz-Weber has a bold and unmistakable voice, preaching the Gospel of Grace in a way the world needs to hear." —*The Orange County Register*

"She is a powerful preacher of grace to those alienated from the church." —*First Things Journal*

"Her book will unsettle the more enculturated Christian but will resonate with many turned off by institutional religion or by a narrow understanding of the Christian faith." —*The Wichita Eagle*

"Her humor and wit come from a recognition of the contradictions, absurdities, and ironies that exist in life." —*The Reading* (PA) *Eagle*

"PASTRIX is littered with colorful characters from Bolz-Weber's life and replete with in-your-face honesty." —*Waterloo-Cedar Falls* (IA) *Courier*

"She's preaching for all the people who tire of the idea of having to pretend to be perfect every Sunday before entering the church doors…And I'm sure if you pick up her book, she'll preach to a few of you." —*The Victoria Advocate*

ALSO BY NADIA BOLZ-WEBER:

*Salvation on the Small Screen?:
24 Hours of Christian Television*

Pastrix

The Cranky,
Beautiful Faith of
a Sinner & Saint

Nadia Bolz-Weber

JERICHO
BOOKS

New York • Boston • Nashville

Copyright © 2013 by Nadia Bolz-Weber

The author is represented by Daniel Literary Group, Nashville, Tennessee.

Scripture quotations are from the New Revised Standard Version Bible, copyright © 1989 National Council of the Churches of Christ in the United States of America. Used by permission. All rights reserved.

"*Pastrix*" definition used by permission of Bryony and Paul Taylor.

Jericho Books
Hachette Book Group
1290 Avenue of the Americas
New York, NY 10104

www.JerichoBooks.com

Printed in the United States of America

LSC-C

Originally published in hardcover by Hachette Book Group.

First trade edition: September 2014

12

Jericho Books is an imprint of Hachette Book Group, Inc.
The Jericho Books name and logo are trademarks of
Hachette Book Group, Inc.

The Hachette Speakers Bureau provides a wide range of authors for speaking events. To find out more, go to www.hachettespeakersbureau.com or call (866) 376-6591.

The publisher is not responsible for websites (or their content) that are not owned by the publisher.

Library of Congress Control Number: 2013938244

ISBN 978-1-4555-2707-6 (pbk.)

For Dick & Peggy

Contents

Nadia Bolz-Weber

pastrix (pas · triks)   noun

1). A term of insult used by unimaginative sections of the church to define female pastors.

2). Female ecclesiastical superhero: Trinity from *The Matrix* in a clerical collar.

"What on earth was that noise?"

"A pastrix just drop-kicked a demon into the seventh circle of hell!"

3). Cranky, beautiful faith of a Sinner & Saint.

—NewWineskinsDictionary.com

Fall 2005

Shit," I thought to myself, "I'm going to be late to New Testament class." The traffic on I-25 in Denver had stopped. Not just slowed to an irritating pace, but fully stopped. For some reason (misanthropy, most likely), I always assume that any traffic stoppage or slowage is due not to construction or an accident, but to human stupidity, as if someone had suddenly forgotten how to drive or decided to stop and pick wildflowers on the interstate.

Attempting to redirect my general disdain for whatever human idiocy has us all stopped on the freeway, and in one of the countless attempts in my life to "be more spiritual," I tried to be present and find something beautiful to distract myself. The beauty of Colorado is something you have to try to actively ignore rather than something you have to try to find, yet so often I forget this. The sky on that day was the kind of clear blue that cannot be replicated or sufficiently described. Most human attempts to recreate this particular blue, while well meaning, are facile. It can only be experienced. And on that fall day, it filled every inch of sky, only occasionally punctuated by a fluffy, little Bob Ross cloud.

The sky was so gorgeous that I rolled down all my windows and leaned forward to try to see more of it out of my windshield. A trucker next to me winked and eyed my tattooed arms—unaware, I'm certain, that the big tattoo covering my forearm was of Saint Mary Magdalene and that I was a Lutheran seminary student, soon to become a Lutheran pastor. Truckers, bikers, and ex-convicts smile at me a lot more than, say, investment bankers do. I smiled back, and then returned my glance to the blue sky above, becoming lost in the thought of the outrageous out-there-ness of space. The beauty of our sky is really just a nice way for the earth to protect us from the terror of what's so vast and unknowable beyond. The boundlessness of the universe is disturbing when you think about it. It's too big and we're too small. Suddenly, in that moment, all I could think was: *What the hell am I doing? Seminary? Seriously? With a universe this vast and unknowable, what are the odds that this story of Jesus is true? Come on, Nadia. It's a fucking fairy tale.*

And in the very next moment I thought this: *Except that throughout my life, I've experienced it to be true.*

I once heard someone say that my belief in Jesus makes them suspect that I intellectually suck my thumb at night. But I cannot pretend, as much as sometimes I would like to, that I have not throughout my life experienced the redeeming, destabilizing love of a surprising God. Even when my mind protests, I still can't deny my experiences. This thing is real to me. Sometimes I experience God when someone speaks the truth to me, sometimes in the moments when I admit I am wrong, sometimes in the loving of someone unlovable, sometimes in reconciliation that feels like it comes from somewhere outside of myself, but almost always when I experience God it comes in the form of some kind of death and resurrection.

The mystery of the universe (the same universe that sometimes still makes me wonder what the hell I'm doing and that maybe this really is a fairy tale) was created by God. And God chose to reveal who God is by slipping into skin and walking among us as Jesus. And the love and grace and mercy of Jesus was so offensive to us that we killed him. The night before this happened Jesus gathered with some real fuck-ups, held up bread and said *take and eat; this is my body for you*. And then he went to the cross. But death could not contain God. God said "yes" to all of our polite "no thank yous" by rising from the dead. Death and resurrection. It is the Christian story as it has been told to me, starting with Mary Magdalene, the first one to tell it; and as it has been confirmed in my experience.

I have only my confession—confession of my own real brokenness and confession of my own real faith to offer in the chapters that follow. My story is not entirely chronological—time often folds in on itself throughout the book—but rather, it's thematic. It is about the development of my faith, the expression of my faith, and the community of my faith. And it is the story of how I have experienced this Jesus thing to be true. How the Christian faith, while wildly misrepresented in so much of American culture, is really about death and resurrection. It's about how God continues to reach into the graves we dig for ourselves and pull us out, giving us new life, in ways both dramatic and small. This faith helped me get sober, and it helped me (is helping me) forgive the fundamentalism of my Church of Christ upbringing, and it helps me to not always have to be right.

Smiley TV preachers might tell you that following Jesus is about being good so that God will bless you with cash and prizes, but really it's much more gruesome and meaningful. It's about spiritual physics. Something has to die for something new to live.

Death and resurrection—the recurring experience of seeing the emptiness, weeping over our inability to fill it or even understand it, and then listening to the sound of God speaking our names and telling God's story—is a messy business. But it's my business, and it's the most beautiful thing I could tell you about.

Early on the first day of the week, **WHILE IT WAS STILL DARK**, Mary Magdalene came to the tomb and saw that the stone had been removed from the tomb. So she ran and went to Simon Peter and the other disciple, the one whom Jesus loved, and said to them, "They have taken the Lord out of the tomb, and we do not know where they have laid him."....But Mary stood weeping outside the tomb. As she wept, she bent over to look into the tomb; and she saw two angels in white, sitting where the body of Jesus had been lying, one at the head and the other at the feet. They said to her, "Woman, why are you weeping?" She said to them, "They have taken away my Lord, and I do not know where they have laid him." When she had said this, she turned round and saw Jesus standing there, but she did not know that it was Jesus. Jesus said to her, "Woman, why are you weeping? For whom are you looking?" Supposing him to be the gardener, she said to him, "Sir, if you have carried him away, tell me where you have laid him, and I will take him away." Jesus said to her, "Mary!" She turned and said to him in Hebrew, "Rabbouni!" (which means Teacher). Jesus said to her, "Do not hold on to me, because I have not yet ascended to the Father. But go to my brothers and say to them, 'I am ascending to my Father and your Father, to my God and your God.'" Mary Magdalene went and announced to the disciples, "I have seen the Lord"; and she told them that he had said these things to her.

CHAPTER 1

The Rowing Team

Blessed are the poor in spirit; for theirs is the kingdom of Heaven.

—*Matthew 5:3*

During my early years of sobriety, I spent most Monday nights in a smoke-filled parish hall with some friends who were also sober alcoholics, drinking bad coffee. Pictures of the Virgin Mary looked down on us, as prayer and despair and cigarette smoke and hope rose to the ceiling. We were a cranky bunch whose lives were in various states of repair. There was Candace, a suburban housewife who was high on heroin for her debutante ball; Stan the depressive poet, self-deprecating and soulful; and Bob the retired lawyer who had been sober since before Jesus was born, but for some reason still looked a little bit homeless.

We talked about God and anger, resentment and forgiveness—all punctuated with profanity. We weren't a ship of fools so much as a rowboat of idiots. A little rowing team, paddling furiously, sometimes for each other, sometimes for ourselves; and when one of us jumped ship, we'd all have to paddle harder.

In 1992, when I started hanging out with the "rowing team," as I began to call them, I was working at a downtown club as a standup comic. I was broken and trying to become fixed and only a few months sober. I couldn't afford therapy, so being paid to be caustic and cynical on stage seemed the next best thing. Plus, I'm funny when I'm miserable.

This isn't exactly uncommon. If you were to gather all the world's comics and then remove all the alcoholics, cocaine addicts, and manic depressives you'd have left…well…Carrot Top, basically. There's something about courting the darkness that makes some people see the truth in raw, twisted ways, as though they were shining a black light on life to illuminate the absurdity of it all. Comics tell a truth you can see only from the underside of the psyche. At its best, comedy is prophesy and societal dream interpretation. At its worst it's just dick jokes.

When I was working as a comic, normal noncomic people would often say, "Wow, I don't know how you can get up in front of all those people with just a microphone." To which I would reply, "Wow, I don't know how you can balance your checkbook and get up for work each day." We all find different things challenging in life. Speaking in front of hundreds of people was far less challenging for me than scheduling dental appointments.

It was almost effortless for me to do comedy, because the underside was where I felt at home—there, everything is marinated in irony and sarcasm until ready to be grilled and handed to a naked emperor. I got regular comedy work, but never went far in the comedy world for several reasons. First, it was because I tended to make the other comics laugh more often than actual audiences, whom I held in contempt (and maybe that's why). Then there was the fact that I wasn't driven to succeed: As soon as it became an effort, I backed off. But the most important reason comedy didn't work for me was that I became healthier and just wasn't that funny anymore. Less miserable = less funny. In the process of becoming sober and trying to rely on God and be honest about my shortcomings, I became willing to show vulnerabilities. This made me easy prey in a comedy club greenroom, which is basically a hotbed of emotional Darwinism, so it wasn't a place I really wanted to spend a whole lot of my free time. In other ways, hanging out with comics could be kind of great. Next to most of them I was the picture of mental health. I befriended—and by befriended I mean occasionally slept with—a wiry-haired, gregarious comic named PJ who had a keen, albeit incredibly perverted, mind. PJ was one of those guys who wasn't exactly GQ material, foregoing well-cut jeans for a regrettable combination of baggy shorts, button-down shirts, and sport sandals.

He had a distinctly feral quality about him that made him seem a bit canine. Despite his almost total lack of style, PJ managed to have a really full social life. He loved women and life and booze and girlie magazines and poker and comedy, not necessarily in that order.

He was also completing his PhD in communications while doing standup, which was made just a tad difficult by his aforementioned vices. One day, I invited him to the rowing team, and he remained a faithful member for the next eight years, often hosting the postmeeting poker games at his house.

If you didn't know PJ well, he didn't seem all that smart, but underneath his foul-mouthed rants was a stunning intellect. His was one of the more filthy acts in Denver, without a lot of highbrow content. He played stupid on stage and he was brilliant at it. I called PJ up once to see how his dissertation was coming along. "Great," he said, "but no one realizes I'm living in my office at the school."

PJ was like one of those cloth dolls with long skirts that you turn upside down and pull the skirt up—and it's no longer granny, but the big bad wolf. The right-side-up doll is a foul-mouthed simpleton, flipped over, a PhD in communications. The right-side-up doll is the fun-loving and charismatic host of a weekly poker game, flipped over, a non-functioning depressive.

PJ was a natural addition to the rowing team, and he infused the meetings with hilarious dark rants. "I wanted to kill myself this morning," PJ would say, "but I thought how much I'd hate providing all you fuckers with a reason to become even more self-absorbed than you already are, so…" He ended most of his sentences with "so…" as if we all knew how to fill in the next blank; if he were to do it for us it wouldn't be as funny. He was someone I wanted to be around, as if his juju would rub off, making me witty and smart and likable like him.

Comedy clubs are closed on Monday nights, but PJ's house was open for Texas Hold'em after our rowing team meetings. I'm pretty sure that when he got sober and removed booze from the equation, he just added extra women and poker and comedy. Mondays at PJ's became a dark carnival of comics, recovering alcoholics, and comics who were recovering alcoholics. Rounds of poker went late into the night, but competitive wit was where the real points were scored. Whenever I could, I would shove aside the inevitable pile of PJ's dirty magazines on the piano bench and sit myself down for a few hours of belly laughing, which was well worth the twenty-five dollars I always lost to them in the process.

Still, underneath the academic success, the adoring comedy club audiences, the many women, and loads of friends, was something corrosive. Eating away at our friend PJ, over the course of a decade, was a force or illness or demon that had staked a corner of PJ's mind, and like the Red Army, marched determinedly, claiming more and more territory each day.

PJ was loved by a lot of people who had no idea how to help him. The rowing team watched over his final years, as his mental illness was tugged and pulled by modern pharmacology but never cured. He'd show up less and less often on

Monday nights, and each time he would be skinnier. It was as though his body began to follow his mind and spirit, which were slowly leaving. He stopped returning our calls.

Several days before he hanged himself, PJ called me. He wanted me to pray for him. It had been ten years since I'd met PJ, and I had since returned to Christianity. I think I was the only religious person he knew. He wondered about God: Was he beyond the pale of God's love? Throwing all my coolness and sarcasm aside, I prayed for him over the phone. I asked that he feel the very real and always available love of God. I prayed that he would know, without reservation, that he was a beloved child of God. I'm sure I said a bunch of other stuff, too. I wanted to be able to cast out this demon that had hold of our PJ, possessing him, telling him lies, and keeping out the light of God's love.

A week and a half later, I was sitting in a huge lecture hall at CU Boulder (where, as a thirty-five-year-old, married mother of two, I was finishing up my undergraduate degree), when my cell phone rang. I rushed outside, the cold air making my eyes water.

Sean, fellow comic and rower said, "Nadia. It's, um...PJ, honey."

"Shit," I said.

"I'm sorry," Sean said. We were all sorry. "Can you do his service?"

This is how I was called to ministry. My main qualification? I was the religious one.

The memorial service took place on a crisp fall day at the Comedy Works club in downtown Denver, with a full house. The alcoholic rowing team and the Denver comics, the comedy club staff and the academics: These were my people. Giving PJ's eulogy, I realized that perhaps I was supposed to be their pastor.

It's not that I felt pious and nurturing. It's that there, in that underground room filled with the smell of stale beer and bad jokes, I looked around and saw more pain and questions and loss than anyone, including myself, knew what to do with. And I saw God. God, right there with the comics standing along the wall with crossed arms, as if their snarky remarks to each other would keep those embarrassing emotions away. God, right there with the woman climbing down the stage stairs after sharing a little too much about PJ being a "hot date." God, among the cynics and alcoholics and queers.

I am not the only one who sees the underside and God at the same time. There are lots of us, and we are at home in the biblical stories of antiheroes and people who don't get it; beloved prostitutes and rough fishermen. How different from that cast of characters could a manic-depressive alcoholic comic be? It was here in the midst of my own community of underside dwellers that I couldn't help but begin to see the Gospel, the life-changing reality that God is not far off, but here among the brokenness of our lives. And having seen it, I couldn't help but point it out. For reasons I'll never quite understand, I realized that I had been called to proclaim the

Gospel from the place where I am, and proclaim where I am from the Gospel.

What had started in early sobriety as a reluctant willingness to start praying again had led to my returning to Christianity, and now had led to something even more preposterous: I was called to be a pastor to my people.

CHAPTER 2

God's Aunt

Let a woman learn in silence with full submission. I permit no woman to teach or to have authority over a man; she is to keep silent.

—*1 Timothy 2:11-12*

Twenty-five years before I would preside at a comedy club funeral, I got baptized. It was a Sunday in the spring of 1981, and I was wearing white sandals. The preacher, in his denim-colored polyester suit, had wound down his sermon and had given an altar call. If you are ready to make your life right with the Lord or if you desire to be baptized, come forward now as we stand and sing.

The people stood and sang, and I walked down the aisle toward the pastor. Another man handed me a card and golf pencil as I sat on the padded pew. After I checked the box indicating that I desired to be baptized, another man approached the pulpit to make the announcement to the congregation. Then I told them which man I wanted to baptize me.

In the church of my childhood it was taught that the "age of accountability" was somewhere around twelve. To hit the age of accountability was to spiritually go off of your parents' insurance. At age twelve the clock starts ticking, spiritually speaking; you know right from wrong now and because of this you are accountable for every time you fuck up. If you sin knowing right from wrong and then die before you chose to be baptized, you burn in hell for eternity. This is when kids start choosing to be baptized. The lag time between entering the age of accountability and having your slate wiped clean through baptism can be terrifying. Many of us would pray not to die in a car crash before we were baptized, like other people pray to not get sick before their employee benefits kick in. Twelve-year-old Church of Christ kids experience a wave of devotion like a Great Awakening comprised only of sixth graders.

Because twelve was the age of accountability, it was also the age at which boys could no longer be taught in Sunday school by women. In accordance with Timothy 2:12, women were not permitted to teach men, therefore a twelve-year-old boy had more authority than a mature woman. Women were not allowed to serve as elders, preachers, or ushers. For some reason, we didn't have the authority to pass a man the collection plate, but we did have the authority to pass the same man a plate of fried chicken and potato salad an hour later at the church potluck.

Dale Douglass was the first man I ever had for a Sunday school teacher. He was soft spoken and funny and parted his full head of thick, sandy-blonde hair so far to the side that it looked like an unnecessary comb-over. Dale started where the woman who taught us the year before (when she still had authority to do so) had left off: testing us to see how many facts we knew about the Bible. I knew a lot of the answers, and it took just three weeks for him to have a special meeting with my parents, at which he informed them they would have to do something about me. I was answering the questions too quickly and it was keeping the boys in the class from having a chance to answer. To their credit, my parents quietly thought this was awesome. They did encourage me to allow space for others, but really they just loved that I knew my Bible and they weren't about to shame me for it.

Precociousness gave way to sarcasm as my ability to analyze the doctrine and social dynamics at church developed. The moment I was able to recognize the difference between what people said (all sex outside of heterosexual marriage is forbidden) and what they did (clandestine affairs with each other) and the difference between what they taught (women were inferior and subordinate to men) and the reality I experienced in the world (then why am I smarter than my Sunday school teacher?), I knew that I had to get out. I was a strong, smart and smart-mouthed girl, and the church I was raised in had no place for that kind of thing even though they loved me.

By the time I left the church, I questioned everything I had ever been told and knew, based on the criteria that I was for sure "not-Christian," but I still didn't manage to be an atheist, as one might expect. I had never stopped believing in God. Not really. But I did have to go hang out with his aunt for a while. She's called the goddess.

My first experience with Wicca was in the mountains west of Denver, on a brown grassy hill above a yurt—a round, nomadic-looking structure inside of which all the lamps were covered with red scarves, making the interior look like an outdoorsy bordello.

I was about twenty years old when my friend Renna (who is as straight as they come) asked if I wanted to go to a lesbian wedding. I replied, "More than anything in the world," so we drove the forty-five minutes listening to the Indigo Girls just to get in the right womany groove, and I held a huge bowl of strawberries on my lap; apparently lesbian weddings are often potluck.

"This is a Wiccan wedding," Renna informed me. I didn't entirely know what that meant, but it sounded "not-Christian," like me, and I suspected that my parents would not approve, and that there would likely be hummus involved, so I was fine with it.

I loved the service and had never seen so many strong women. Women with shoulders back and hair shorn tight and nothing to hide. We stood in a circle and sang some simple chants, and the brides were so happy, like any other brides, only these two wore Renaissance fair–style garb and were marrying each other. There was talk of perfect love and perfect trust, and we fed each other bread and wine saying, "May you never hunger and may you never thirst." It felt like communion.

There was something safe about being around women. They let me hang out with God's aunt, and I couldn't help but think she liked me. I spent a few years with these women, marking the seasons and sharing our lives, and always there were potlucks. We talked of relationships and pregnancies that didn't last and bosses and roommates that didn't appreciate us and how much garlic to add to vegan salad dressing. At one month's potluck every one of us brought dessert and no one thought that was a problem.

There was no doctrine. We never talked about belief, we just shared our lives and spoke of the divine feminine in ourselves and in the world. The goddess we spoke of never felt to me like a substitute for God, but simply another aspect of the divine. Just like God's aunt.

When I tell other Christians of my time with the goddess, I think they expect me to characterize it as a period in my life when I was misguided, and that I have now thankfully come back to both Jesus and my senses. But it's not like that. I can't imagine that the God of the universe is limited to our ideas of God. I can't imagine that God doesn't reveal God's self in countless ways outside of the symbol system of Christianity. In a way, I need a God who is bigger and more nimble and mysterious than what I could understand and contrive. Otherwise it can feel like I am worshipping nothing more than my own ability to understand the divine.

In fact, I felt guided by God the whole time I sojourned outside of the church. The divine source of my life and my identity perhaps knew that I needed to bask in a female face of God for a good long while outside the church before I ever could return to it whole and be able see the divine feminine in my own tradition. If feminist scholar Mary Daly was right, that "If God is male, then male is God," then there was some undoing to be done inside of myself after a childhood of being told that God is male and I am not (but sixth grade Jimmy over there is!).

Much later, in my mid-thirties and after PJ died, was when I realized that what I really wanted, more than anything, was to be a pastor to my people—preferably young, urban, smart-asses who wanted something more than the categories of late-stage capitalism to tell them who they are—I had, through the right combination of time, sobriety, and therapy, ceased being angry about the fundamentalism of my childhood. But there was one problem with my being a pastor: I'm a lousy candidate. I swear like a truck driver, I'm covered in tattoos, and I'm kind of selfish. Nothing about me says "Lutheran pastor."

So I was scared. I was scared about the fact that in order for me to be the kind of pastor I would want to be, I would need to look at some of my own personal stuff, which I was perfectly happy ignoring. I struggled with the idea of being a spiritual leader. I struggled with knowing I don't really like emotionally needy people and, given the opportunity, I will walk the other way if I see them coming. I struggled with being available to people all the time when really I'm slightly misanthropic. I struggled with many things, but, despite my upbringing, what I didn't struggle with was my gender. My calling to be a pastor, while still shocking, had become less and less ambiguous and even started to feel precious to me. That's why I didn't want tell my parents.

I was experiencing a feeling of purpose, perhaps for the first time in my life, and the last thing I wanted was for them to squash it. And yet, they had to know at some point, so on a Saturday in November of 2005, I sat in my parents' living room on their brocade, overstuffed sofa, and while they stared at the brand-new tattoo of Mary Magdalene that now covered my forearm, I confessed, and not very elegantly.

"I...um...am really enjoying seminary, and I need to tell you that I've changed my degree track from an academic degree to a pastoral degree. Umm...see...I feel like maybe God is calling me to start a church, and I guess I think maybe I'm supposed to be a pastor to my people, but I'm scared, and well...I am...but..." I had no idea if any of it made sense, but it was being spoken. I was terrified that they would reject the idea and shame me for my disregard for the scriptures, which forbid a woman to teach. And I wasn't sure what felt worse: the possibility of them shaming me or the fact that they still could.

At that moment, my father silently stood up, walked to the bookshelf and took down his worn, leather-bound Bible. Here we go, I thought, he's going to beat me with the scripture stick.

He opened it up and read. I could tell from where he was

turning that it wasn't one of Paul's letters at the end of the book, but something closer to the middle. My father did not read the 1st Timothy passage about women being silent in church. He read from Esther.

From my father I heard only these words: "But you were born for such a day as this." He closed the book and my mother joined him in embracing me. They prayed over me and they gave me a blessing. And some blessings, like the one my conservative Christian parents gave to their soon-to-be-Lutheran pastor daughter who had put them through hell, are the kind of blessings that stay with you for the rest of your life. The kind you can't speak of without crying all over again.

CHAPTER 3

Albion Babylon

Circa 1988

They should fix that light," my older sister Barbara said. The long fluorescent lights in the dingy basement hallway, which led to the two-bedroom, garden-level apartment I now shared with seven roommates, flickered in and out like a strobe, making our walk to the third apartment on the right look deceptively short.

My sister and I had been close most of my life, and she had agreed to hang out with me as I moved into this squalid apartment. I'd recently dropped out of college after a single semester and had very little, whereas Barb was getting her PhD in English at Indiana University and owned things like a washer and dryer. At nineteen, in the winter of 1988, I owned a single apple crate of essential possessions: a worn copy of *The Farm Vegetarian Cookbook*, my combat boots, an old mannequin head, and several important cassette tapes: *Ziggy Stardust, Violent Femmes, Road to Ruin.*

The Ramones. I was twelve years old when I bought *Road to Ruin* from Big Apple Tapes & Records across from the caramel corn stand in the Mall of the Bluffs in Colorado Springs. Until that day, there had been only Jim Croce, John Denver, and the Kingston Trio in our middle-class Christian home. But now those guys, with their mustaches and mildness, had to step aside for four boys from Queens because I had spent all my allowance money on the Ramones' *Road to Ruin*. And every afternoon for weeks I sat in my Holly Hobbie bedroom playing that record over and over on my plastic orange and white Fisher-Price record player while I stared at the album cover. Hoping that maybe Joey and Dee Dee Ramone would magically show up at my house in their ripped Levi's and leather jackets and take me away. The anger of punk rock felt custom made for me.

At the time I began my love affair with the Ramones, my parents didn't know that I was buying punk rock records, just like they didn't know that I was stealing food at school. Teachers at my junior high school would leave snacks on their desks, and I was so hungry that I'd take their granola bars and baggies of crackers, not because there wasn't enough food at home, there was, I just couldn't get enough to eat no matter what I packed in my lunch or packed in my mouth.

I was eleven when I slowly started weighing less and eating more. And my parents, Dick and Peggy, with their love and can-do attitude, just thought it was due to a growth spurt and encouraged me to be proud of my height and stand up straight. The next year, when my handwriting was so terrible that my grades were crashing, my mom bought me a lovely calligraphy set hoping to inspire some pride in my penmanship. And when I became pale and lethargic, my mother thought some fresh Colorado air might be in order and took me cross-country skiing, which was the day she realized something more was wrong than could be fixed with discipline and optimism. I slept in the backseat of our Chevy Citation on the way to the mountains, the movement of a stick-shifted Chevy causing my gut to lurch. Later, when we had finally gotten geared up and started skiing, the weight of my wool sweater felt like one of those lead X-ray aprons and my legs just wouldn't move, so I finally insisted that we leave. Plus I'd already eaten all of the snacks. When we got home my mother made a doctor's appointment.

What I had was Graves' disease. It is a thyroid-related auto-immune disorder, which causes many delightful things to happen in one's body: rapid heart rate, hand tremors, pale skin, increased metabolism, lethargy, mania, depression, and sensitivity to heat. It's like methamphetamine without the part that feels good. Oh, and it's free.

The disease had caused fatty tissue to build up behind my eyes, forcing them to protrude out of their sockets. The sphere of my eyeball bulged so far out of my head that my eyelids could no longer close. White was visible all the way around the iris, as though I had just received an electric shock or seen something terrifying…only I looked like that all the time.

All the time.

From age twelve to sixteen. Every day of my life.

Mom would drive me to Denver to see eye specialists on a monthly basis, so they could make sure my corneas weren't damaged (I'd started sleeping with a salve in my eyes to prevent them from drying out) but also so that they could keep measuring the bones in my face. The bug-eyed thing could be corrected with surgery. But not until the bones in my face stopped growing. And it ends up that you can't make the bones in your face stop growing through discipline or optimism.

Most junior high kids think they look like insects. I actually did. So most days on the school bus, I would spend the twenty-minute ride pressing my palms over my eyes, thinking that were I just determined and consistent enough in my efforts, I could force my eyes back. But it just doesn't work like that. Kids can't wish hard enough that their divorced parents get back together and they can't make themselves good enough students to make their manic-depressive mother stop being crazy and they can't force their bug-eyes back into their eye sockets by twenty minutes of pushing on them on a school bus ride. But that has never stopped kids from trying.

It's unclear if every school bus in America is installed with its own bully in the backseat as standard equipment, along with a fire extinguisher and the driver's silver-elbow door lever, but it sure felt like that. My standard-issue bully was not that special: a larger-than-the-other-girls chick named Becky, who had feathered hair and wore Def Leppard T-shirts.

She noticed my palms over my eyes, and when she called

it to attention, I lied. "What the hell are you doing?" Becky asked with a sneer. "Trying to fix your bug-eyes?"

"I'm meditating," I said. "Buddhist." And then I sat with my skinny legs crossed on the bus bench.

The next day I just wore sunglasses.

Eventually I'd begin to walk the low-ceilinged halls of Horace Mann Junior High School with my eyes squinted and not looking directly at anyone, the way the girls who developed early held their Trapper Keepers in front of their chests. I may have averted my eyes, but I never dropped my chin. Not once.

Everyone has their own middle school horror story. It's a trial by fire, and the person we will become can usually be traced back to seventh grade. But everyone reacts to their middle school experiences uniquely. For me, what I was developing in those low-ceilinged hallways was more than just a "problem with anger," as it would later be called. The daily barrage of malicious language spat my way from Becky and others made me angry, and yet somehow the anger protected me. That protection took the form of cynicism and a heightened awareness of people's bullshit. I began to smell it out like a drug dog in a Colombian airport.

Church, for all its faults, was the only place outside of my own home where people didn't gawk at me or make fun of me. I could go to church and be greeted with my actual name and not a taunt. I could go to church and be part of the youth group. I could go to church and no one stared. Which is why it sucked that there were other reasons I'd eventually not fit in.

Belonging to the Church of Christ—and therefore, being a Christian—mostly meant being really good at *not* doing things. Not drinking, obviously, not being snarky and sarcastic, not having sex outside of marriage, not smoking, not dancing, not swearing, not dating people outside the church and, of course, perhaps most important of all, no mixed bathing. The better you were at not doing these things, the better a Christian you were. It did not seem to me, even back then, that God's grace or the radical love of Jesus was what united people in the Church of Christ; it was their ability to be good. Or at least their ability to appear to be good. And not everyone can pull that off.

So while I was accepted at church despite my bug-eyes, the rage and cynicism I had developed as a result of those bug-eyes was decidedly "not Christian." My newfound appreciation for the word "bullshit," for example, was not Christian. Sarcasm was not Christian. Punk rock proved there were other people out there who also wanted to scream and break shit, which changed my life, but punk rock, screaming, and breaking shit was also…not Christian. That is to say, *I* was not Christian.

I continued on the unchristianlike track when, six months before I had the surgery to correct my eyes, I started drinking. Fast forward four years, and I was a no-longer-bug-eyed nineteen-year-old with purple hair, a drinking problem, an attitude problem, and a smoking-pot-every-day problem.

Most of my peers were in college by then, an endeavor at which I had tried and then quickly failed after only four months. I had succeeded in impressing the frat boys with my ability to drink "like a man," but I had not succeeded in actually showing up for class, and only later did it dawn on me that perhaps these two things were related.

Having graduated from high school with a 2.0 GPA, I had basically sweet-talked my way into Pepperdine University. It was technically a Church of Christ school, but being located in California and not in a proper Christian state like Texas or Tennessee, it was suspect among traditionalists. Given the church's feelings about "mixed bathing"—boys and girls in the same swimming pool at the same time—they probably thought locating a Church of Christ school in the beach community of Malibu was like locating an Amish boarding school on the strip in Vegas.

After my brief college career, I went back to Denver. I'd been there a few months and was washing dishes part-time in an upscale Mexican restaurant with marginal food when I met Scotty, a long-torsoed, big-hearted nineteen-year-old pothead with an apartment on Albion Street where he said that anyone could stay. Within a week, Barb was helping me move in.

From the open front door on the night I moved in, my sister pointed to the unwashed kitchen counter, a huge green bong, a bedroom with three mattresses on the floor, and a guy asleep on a torn sofa. "Honey," she whispered, "really?"

I thought to myself, *We're not all cut out for graduate school, Barb.*

The apartment quickly became my home, the people there my ersatz community. We shared our drugs and tried to make sure everyone was fed. Before I had arrived, someone had slapped a blue and yellow "Just Say No" sticker on the four-foot-long fiberglass bong in the living room; it rested along a nicotine-stained wall on which a "Reaganstein" poster hung (Ronald Reagan: green, bolts in head, arms raised). No one did much cooking in the apartment, other than boiling the occasional packet of ramen. (And once someone cooked a rattlesnake; a drunken endeavor designed to thrill roommates and defy convention. It rotted before someone, not I, was thoughtful enough to throw it out.) We called our filthy home Albion Babylon.

On my first night at Albion Babylon, I unpacked my possessions, soon realizing that the apple box was the only thing I had to put my things into, so I set it on its side like a little hutch, and piled everything up inside it as neatly as I could. I took out a black marker, drew a circle around the apple and couldn't decide whether to make it into a peace sign or an anarchy sign. Peace. No...anarchy. I tried both together and it just looked like some kind of insignia from Star Trek. I covered the old mattress on the floor with a cheery yellow flowered bedsheet and my duvet. I was so grateful to have a place to sleep that didn't come with expectations like my parents' house or my dorm at Pepperdine or, for the love of God, the Church of Christ.

Yet for all its nonsense and obsession with being good and alienation of people who weren't their particular *brand* of "good," the Church of Christ I was raised in was a community. As churchgoers, our lives were shared. We gathered for worship with a congregation of people three times a week to sing and pray and share communion. And throughout the rest of the week we hung out with people from church. My parents' home in particular was one of the popular hangout spots. People were always eating at our table, sleeping on our sofas, and studying the Bible in our living room.

Once, a young couple showed up at our doorstep. "We're friends of the Slaters from Detroit and we're driving through Denver. They said we might be able to stay here."

"Pull up a sofa," my parents would say. "Here's a couple of towels. Will you give me a hand peeling carrots?"

That was our home and it was kind of beautiful. But like every other kid on the planet, I didn't understand that my family was weird until much later in life. Unlike my feelings toward the Christian fundamentalism from which I would soon part ways, I never stopped valuing the spiritual weirdness of hospitality and community. And without realizing it, I spent the next ten years trying to recreate a spiritual community of my own. Only I was looking for a community in which *all* of me would actually fit.

So I was thrilled to have found Albion Babylon. We felt like a community. We laughed a lot in our garden-level apartment, and drank competitively and didn't often leave the apartment. Scotty, the guy from the Mexican restaurant, had already done a stint in rehab. Once he shared with me a book he made, a brown scrapbook sort of thing with photos and drawings and writings. It was a self-awareness project he was forced to do in treatment, but in which he now hid his dope. I loved him for his poems and pictures and for keeping pot inside his in-patient memento. It felt like a fuck you to his parents who were "so concerned" about him.

I made a book like his: a drawing, a bad poem, a list of my heroes, my faults and my strengths. Heroes: (1) Jesus Christ, (2) Che Guevara. Strength: humor. Fault: running away. I wrote that Jesus was a real revolutionary and that Christianity had unfortunately given the guy a bad name. At nineteen, my goals were to travel more, to live in a commune or intentional community of some sort, and to contribute to world peace through revolutionary action.

We eventually picked up two more roommates and decided to move into a rental house, a blond brick ranch house on Humboldt Street near the Iliff School of Theology campus— an institution I'd eventually attend, but, at the time, I didn't even notice. In our new home, the Humboldt House, we all felt free from the constraints of convention and being parented, and we had a yard.

My friends and I now had a proper home, and while the slightly toothless guy from Alabama created hydroponic grow rooms for the dope, I decided to take on more traditional home-making practices. Knowing nothing about bread baking or vege-table gardening, I tried my hand at both: the results of both being dry and sandy. I would throw seeds at the dry ground thinking we would be fed by the results. No food grew. And I was still hungry. I also decorated the edge of the linoleum floor in my base-ment bedroom with my empty vodka bottles which were end-lessly being kicked over by my roommates and their boyfriends and girlfriends (whom I would "accidentally" sleep with).

On some Sunday mornings, when I was able to shake off the hangover, and without really knowing why, I would sneak off to a nearby Quaker meeting, which was a liberal church where no one said anything. Their worship service was an experience in shared silence, so there was no preaching and no men going on endlessly in show-offy prayers. Sitting in the oak-planked pews with a community of people felt reassuring and familiar; plus, I appreciated not being told what to do to be good. The people who sat around me on those silent mornings grew actual gardens and protested wars and read the *New York Times*. They were kind and never mentioned the smell coming off of me from not having totally metabolized all the alcohol from the night before.

Still, although the Quakers were a community, I wasn't really part of it. I was more of a spectator. My community was down the street still sleeping it off. But things were starting to fall apart at our house. People were getting sloppy. One guy now had a gun, and our redneck roommate started to sell speed and more and more strangers were showing up. No one cared about gardening. I didn't actually care about gardening. We all just did whatever we wanted. Everyone disappointed me, and I baked bread only that one time.

Turns out, what I wanted was to be in a community with people who wouldn't, say, disassemble the engine of a 1981 Honda Civic and leave it in the living room for four months. People who, if their tomcat peed on my duvet, would consider neutering the cat or at least offering to pay the dry cleaning bill. They wouldn't just use it as an opportunity to inform me, glassy-eyed, of how uptight I am and that people really have no right to manipulate the reproductive systems of other animals...man. And perhaps more than anything, I wanted to be in a community with those who could not only love a once bug-eyed girl, but also could reliably flush the toilet. And hell, perhaps they wanted to have a roommate who didn't sleep with their boyfriends and girlfriends.

We had started out caring about each other, but in the end none of us knew how to care *for* each other. But this experience taught me that a community based on the idea that everyone hates rules is, in the end, just as disappointing and oppressive as a community based on the ability to follow rules.

I moved out two weeks before the cops busted the house.

Early on the first day of the week, while it was still dark, Mary Magdalene came to the tomb and saw that the stone had been removed from the tomb. So she ran and went to Simon Peter and the other disciple, the one whom Jesus loved, and said to them, "They have taken the Lord out of the tomb, and we do not know where they have laid him." . . . But Mary stood weeping outside the tomb. As she wept, she bent over to look into the tomb; and she saw two angels in white, sitting where the body of Jesus had been lying, one at the head and the other at the feet. They said to her, "Woman, why are you weeping?" She said to them, "They have taken away my Lord, and I do not know where they have laid him." When she had said this, she turned round and saw Jesus standing there, but she did not know that it was Jesus. Jesus said to her, "Woman, why are you weeping? For whom are you looking?" Supposing him to be the gardener, she said to him, "Sir, if you have carried him away, tell me where you have laid him, and I will take him away." Jesus said to her, "Mary!" She turned and said to him in Hebrew, "Rabbouni!" (which means Teacher). Jesus said to her, "Do not hold on to me, because I have not yet ascended to the Father. But go to my brothers and say to them, 'I am ascending to my Father and your Father, to my God and your God.'" Mary Magdalene went and announced to the disciples, "I have seen the Lord"; and she told them that he had said these things to her.

CHAPTER 4

La Femme Nadia

I do not understand my own actions. For I do not do what I want, but I do the very thing I hate.

—*Romans 7:15*

The Sunday after New Year's Day 1992, I was six days sober and sitting in a dingy, generic room filled with cigarette smoke and sober women—suburban housewives, haggard cocktail waitresses, a couple of grandmas, and a lawyer—on the second floor of York Street. York Street is an old Victorian house that is being used as a center for alcoholism recovery meetings in Denver. The grandeur of the home had faded after over twenty years of continually being used as a meeting space for sober drunks. The grand wraparound porch, which long ago hosted corseted Victorian ladies and cummerbunded gentlemen, was now dotted with half-full butt cans, homeless men, and attorneys briskly sliding into their Audis to avoid being seen at a recovery center by colleagues or clients who may be driving on actual York Street.

You used to be able to smoke at York Street, but only on the second floor, and smoking is helpful when you are shaky from not drinking and dubious about the prospect of recovery in the first place. I wasn't at all sure this thing was going to work for me or that I belonged at York Street or that any of these women had ever gone through what I was going through. But I did know that I didn't like any of them.

As we sat in a circle on the second floor, they talked about God, blah blah blah, and surrender, blah blah blah, and I didn't buy it. My skin felt like the rough side of Velcro, and every sound was tearing away at my nerves. My right foot was furiously bouncing my leg up and down like it was its job. I thought of my sober friend Nora, who once said that if she weren't an alcoholic she'd be drunk every day. I smiled at how much that made sense. What I really wanted was a couple shots of vodka, but what I had was six days of sobriety and what now seemed like a nervous disorder.

While the lawyer spoke, my mind wandered to a week before, when on Christmas Day I had started drinking at ten a.m. and woke up twenty-four hours later in the bed of a line cook from the restaurant where I worked—whom I had no memory of either hanging out with or ever being attracted to. But the thing that horrified me was not that I had drank so much that I had ended up in a strange house with little memory of the evening before. I had engaged in the consistently stupid for quite a while at that point: getting tattooed in a junkie's living room, snorting cocaine in the bathroom of Nell's in New York, crashing my motorcycle on a patch of ice (not being sober enough to consider that maybe winter isn't motorcycle season). Instead, what was horrifying that Christmas Day was that none of it horrified me.

If my poor mother had known even a small piece of it, she would have never recovered, but I had acted as if it was all just a part of my starring role in Andrew Lloyd Webber's version of *Nadia,* and wasn't I fabulous? I carried a bravado about my drinking like I was a hero of debauchery. But on that Christmas Day, it felt like shit. I had a vague realization that I was just trying to keep up with some version of myself that I had decided was accurate.

I assumed I'd be dead by thirty. I'm not certain of the exact origins of the idea, but I'm guessing it was a biopic about Jim Morrison. Or maybe it was *Sid and Nancy.* Whatever Hollywood movie I had absorbed and decided was "me," the fact is that it took me years to become willing to rethink this idea of myself. The idea that I was slightly out of control (but in a charming way) and would die young had become like a favorite outfit I refused to vary because I liked how I looked in it. And at first this was exhilarating. As a teenager, I loved how I looked in the outfit of using drugs and exercising poor judgment. I had tried it on, spun around in the mirror, and decided I would choose this look, this image, this identity. But eventually and without my realizing it, the ability to choose had gone. I had become what at first I had only pretended to be.

When you can't control something—like how if I take one drink all bets are off no matter what motivation I have for controlling myself—it's easier to arrange a life in which it looks like you've chosen it all, as opposed to facing the truth: You have lost your ability to choose any of it.

On December 26, 1991, six days before the meeting I was sitting in now, I showed up to my first twelve-step meeting to prove to my friend Sandra that no, I wasn't an alcoholic. Sandra was a semiprofessional con artist who made a lot of our drinking money ripping off old people by selling them more hearing aids than they needed. She was my most recent drinking partner and had been in and out of recovery programs for the last six years.

We were on our fourth round at Ms C's, a lesbian country and western bar, when she blurted out, "Girl, I gotta try to sober up again." Her face was swollen from a bender, and at the time I thought to myself, *Quitter*. "And seriously Nadia," she continued, "you're a fucking alcoholic."

I wanted to prove her wrong and maybe also get some tips on how to just control myself a little so I could enjoy my drinking without the bother of vomiting. So the next day, I sat pretentiously on an old sofa in the corner of a church basement, certain everyone in the room knew I was not supposed to be there. Now it was six days later, and my leg wouldn't stop twitching. I was still looking for an affirmation that I wasn't an alcoholic, so that, dear Jesus, I could go drink again.

Margery, a leather-faced woman with a New Jersey accent, was talking about prayer or some other nonsense when suddenly a sound like a pan falling on a tile floor came up from the kitchen below us. I jerked out of my seat like I was avoiding shrapnel, but no one else reacted. Without skipping half a beat, Margery turned to me, with a long slim cigarette in her hand and said, "Honey, that'll pass." She took a drag and went on, "So anyways, prayer is…"

In that moment I realized that, because of how immediately she turned to me and said this, Margery knew what it meant to be shaky from not taking a drink, knew that it apparently was temporary, and she maybe even knew how to keep from drinking, even though it sucked so much. I was in the right place. I started, very gradually, to go to these meetings and listen to old broads like Margery. Even when they started talking about God.

And these people talked about God a lot. But never about an angry God who judged or condemned or was always disappointed in people. The God they spoke of was not the God I was taught to fear.

"You just have to find a higher power you can do business with," Margery suggested one morning when I admitted that I hated Christianity. "This isn't about religion, honey."

For her, God was the key to staying sober. Her relationship to God wasn't doctrinal. It was functional.

"Just stop thinking about it so damned much. When you get up in the morning ask God to help keep you sober, and before you go to sleep thank him." I cringed at the male pronoun, but that night, I did it anyway.

You know those friendships where time and distance are

irrelevant, and you can pick up where you left off even after years of not talking? My relationship with God wasn't like that. It wasn't that I didn't believe in God. I had never managed to actually be an atheist. I believed there was something in the universe, some great creative force that bound everything together. Something I was connected to. I liked to call it spirit and goddess, and now and again I was willing to maybe call it God, as long as Christianity stayed out of it. Still, talking to God felt like I was starting from scratch.

I went almost every day to those meetings at York Street and in various church basements. I'd sit in metal folding chairs on linoleum floors and drink light-brown coffee out of Styrofoam cups while sober drunks would speak of God, often simply as their higher power. The lack of theological specificity was perhaps the only thing that enabled me to keep showing up. But once in that first six months, I was sitting in a twelve-step meeting in an upstairs room of a Masonic lodge when someone shared about something he had read in the Bible that week that really spoke to his sobriety.

I stood up and walked out. The Bible had been the weapon of choice in the spiritual gladiatorial arena of my youth. I knew how, wielded with intent and precision, the Bible can cut deeply, while the one holding it can claim with impunity that "this is from God." Apparently if God wrote the Bible (a preposterous idea), then any verse used to exclude, shame, harm, or injure another person is not only done in the name of God, but also out of love and concern for the other person. I had been that person on several occasions, lying spiritually bleeding on the ground, while the nice, well-meaning, and concerned Christians stood above me and smiled in condescension, so pleased with themselves that they had "spoken the truth in love."

The book that God "wrote" had been used to hurt me and others, so when someone mentioned it in a twelve-step meeting, that was all I could think of. And if I had to find "a God I could do business with," as Margery put it, it wouldn't be the guy who wrote a book like the Bible. Who knew that later I would come to love the Bible, once I discovered all the amazing parts no one ever talked about when I was growing up.

But the connection—the deep, ongoing, and personal connection people like Margery had with God, a power greater than their alcoholic selves—was in no way based in piety or righteousness. It was based solely on something I could relate to a hell of a lot more: desperation.

When I look back on it now, I see it all as an interruption. It was as if God abruptly, even rudely, interrupted my life. I had been fine with trying to attain a rock-and-roll early death. I thought it was hilarious that I would show up for my waitressing job with rashes on my face from having fallen asleep in a puddle of my own vodka vomit. All the times I had said that I should really try to stop drinking were just a way of saying *look at how good I am at being a drunk*, which was just a way of saying, *aren't I an adorable mess?*

So when I stopped drinking, when I stopped going to bars every night and instead went to church basements, it felt like it was not a matter of will. It was against my will, actually, and

I was furious about it. I seethed about having had booze taken away from me when it was the one thing I could rely on to even slightly loosen those muscles in my chest that knot up from the fear and pressure of just being human.

But I kept going and I kept not drinking and I kept listening to women like Margery, because in those rooms, I heard truth spoken. Despite my desire to just learn how to drink like a lady, I stuck around to learn from these people about how folks like us manage to stay sober. I had heard the familiar truth of my own drinking problem coming out the mouths of old men and street punks and lawyers and old dames like Margery, enough that to deny it would take a stronger act of will than to just surrender myself to it.

I relate it to that great French film *Le Femme Nikita* (and later a lousy American remake, *Point of No Return*), from the early 1990s. Nikita was a teenage drug addict and the sole survivor of a police standoff with her band of thieves. The government faked her death, put her in prison, and then gave her the option to occupy the grave in which she was supposed to be lying or work for them, quid pro quo.

Getting sober never felt like I had pulled myself up by my own spiritual bootstraps. It felt instead like I was on one path toward self-destruction and God pulled me off of it by the scruff of my collar, me hopelessly kicking and flailing and saying, "Screw you. I'll take the destruction please." God looked at tiny, little red-faced me and said, "that's adorable," and then plunked me down on an entirely different path. I am like a Lutheran Nikita. I was allowed not to die in exchange for working for God. I'd get a life back, a rich one I'd never have chosen out of a catalog, a life where I would marry a nice man, go to college, have a couple babies, attend seminary, become ordained as a Lutheran Pastor, and start a church. I'd get my life back, but eventually I'd have to work for God. I'd have to become God's bitch.

CHAPTER 5

Thanks, ELCA!

For the kingdom of heaven is like a landowner who went out early in the morning to hire laborers for his vineyard...And about five o'clock he went out and found others standing around; and he said to them, "Why are you standing here idle all day?" They said to him, "Because no one has hired us."
—*Matthew 20:1, 6-7a*

On the first date with my husband, I asked if he was a unicorn. It felt like an honest question.

By the time I met Matthew, it had been a decade since I'd left the church of my youth, during which time I became increasingly aware of injustice and poverty and the basic horrors of society, which I felt could only be ignored by the most heartless of people. I had never heard anything about caring for the poor in the church of my childhood. We were more of a "just over in the glory land" kind of crowd who set our sights on heaven above.

I thought I had moved as far from the fundamentalism of my childhood as possible. But at the time I didn't know that it would take more to escape black-and-white thinking than just no longer attending your parents' church. The church had provided me a sorting system, which was now ingrained. It had containers into which every person and idea and event was to be placed. These were sometimes labeled "saved" and "not saved" (those who will join us in the glory land and those who will not) or perhaps "us" and "not us" (same thing) or simply just "good" and "bad" (again, same thing). As a teenager, I began to question the Great Christian Sorting System. My gay friends in high school were kind and funny and loved me, so I suspected that my church had placed them in the wrong category. And dancing, it turns out, was fun. Swimming in the same pool with boys was normal (and fun), and in the end, people who weren't Christians, to me, just felt easier to be around. Injustices in the world needed to be addressed and not ignored. Christians weren't good; people who fought for peace and justice were good. I had been lied to, and in my anger at being lied to about the containers, I left the church. But it turns out, I hadn't actually escaped the sorting system. I had just changed the labels.

I began to realize this when, in January 1995, I met Matthew, a tall, really cute Lutheran seminary student. We met playing a game of pickup volleyball. (Volleyball courts, after all, are the sacred breeding grounds of tall people.)

I had been sober for four years and was still hanging out with

God's aunt at the time I went out with Matthew. I was also in therapy with a middle-aged therapist who wore flowing clothes and sang in some sort of choir. She was smart and seemed to be genuinely optimistic about me in a way that made me question her judgment while also being desperately grateful to her. I nervously mentioned one day in the spring of 1995 that I had met a really cute guy, but that he was…um…nice. This obviously was a problem (a previous boyfriend had spent six years in San Quentin for armed robbery), so "nice" had never been a compelling characteristic to me. "Why don't you just try it?" she offered. Best seventy-five dollars I ever spent, that hour of therapy.

On our first date, Matthew and I sat across the booth from each other at el Taco de Mexico, one of the only places in Denver where you can get brain tostadas and tongue tacos. Over two plates of less adventurous chile relleno burritos, Matthew asked me about my interests. We spoke of social issues: racism, homelessness, and women's rights, and we saw eye to eye on everything. Then he said, "Well, my heart for social justice is rooted in my Christian faith."

Um, what? I just stared at him, saying nothing. He went on to tell me that he was a Lutheran seminary student at Iliff School of Theology, and that he was in the peace and social justice–focused master of divinity program; he was in school to be a Lutheran pastor. Oh, yeah, and he was from Texas. Like I said, Matthew was a unicorn; a mythical combination of creatures that doesn't exist in reality.

But I soon learned that there was actually a whole world of Christians who take Matthew 25 seriously, who believe that when we feed the hungry, clothe the naked, and care for the sick, we do so to Jesus' own self. They weren't magical fantasy creatures, they were just a kind of Christian I had never heard of. I thought that was interesting and quaint, but still, not for me. My own internal sorting system wouldn't allow for it; if I started to put some Christians in the "good" container where would it end? Still, the date with the Lutheran unicorn went well enough that six months later we were living together in Oakland, where we had moved so Matthew could finish his Lutheran seminary training. While in California, I spent several months trying like hell to be a Unitarian. Quakerism didn't work for me, Wicca was great, but I always felt like I was just visiting. So I hoped Unitarianism would be just right. Unitarians are such smart, good people. They seem so hopeful. They vote Democrat and recycle and love women and they let you believe anything you want to, and I wanted to be one of them badly. But I couldn't pull it off. Four years of sobriety hadn't come to me as a result of hopefulness and positive thinking. It was grace. Unitarians just don't talk much about our need for God's grace. They have a higher opinion of human beings than I have ever felt comfortable claiming, as someone who both reads the paper and knows the condition of my own heart. Having had the experience of getting sober and feeling like God interrupted my bullshit life, I couldn't be comforted by my own divinity or awesomeness, although I'd love it if I could. In the end, as much as I desperately wanted to be Unitarian, I couldn't, because what I needed was a specific divine source of reconciliation and wholeness, a source that is connected to me in love, but does not come from inside of me.

One morning, I sat in our tiny apartment kitchen lamenting over a bowl of oatmeal how un-Unitarian I was, when Matthew said, "Just come with me to St. Paul's on Sunday. It doesn't suck, I promise. Plus you'll love Pastor Ross; he's gay." I relented, but only because the pastor was gay, and I hoped that meant some flamboyance and dramatics.

As Matthew drove us the following Sunday to St. Paul Lutheran Church in Oakland, I asked him a slew of slightly anxious questions like, "Can I sit on the aisle in case I need to escape?" By the time we arrived I had calmed down and actually convinced myself that it was going to be just like Culture Club meets the 700 Club. But it was just a church. And yet it wasn't at all just a church. There were no dramatics or drag. Just a whole lot of people who didn't seem to really match each other: gay, straight, kids, elderly folks in wheelchairs, white, black. The building was old and respectable, with red carpeting and dark wood. I sat on the end of an old pew and took in the beautiful stained glass.

I had never experienced liturgy before. But here the congregation said things together during the service. And they did stuff: stood, sat, knelt, crossed themselves, went up to the altar for communion, like choreographed sacredness.

In the car on the way home I asked Matthew, "So if I go back, and I'm not saying I will, but if I do, will they do those same things and say those same things again next week?" He grinned. "Yes, Nadia. That's what we call 'liturgy.' People have been doing those things and saying those things for a couple millennia, and I'm pretty sure...next week, too."

It was in those first couple months that I fell in love with liturgy, the ancient pattern of worship shared mainly in the Catholic, Lutheran, Orthodox, and Episcopal churches. It felt like a gift that had been caretaken by generations of the faithful and handed to us to live out and caretake and hand off. Like a stream that has flowed long before us and will continue long after us. A stream that we get to swim in, so that we, like those who came before us, can be immersed in language of truth and promise and grace. Something about the liturgy was simultaneously destabilizing and centering; my individualism subverted by being joined to other people through God to find who I was. Somehow it happened through God. One specific, divine force.

I didn't really know the hymns though. And several of them just seemed unfortunate. Four months later, on the Sunday Matthew and I announced our engagement, I stood during the closing hymn with everyone else even though I wasn't singing. As the crucifer (the person in the procession and recession who holds the crucifix) passed me, I saw behind him Pastor Ross, who started to grin. As he approached me, he quickly leaned over, bright eyed, and whispered, "Now, Nadia, pastor's wives are expected to sing *all* the verses of the hymn." He winked and kept walking.

One Sunday, Pastor Ross announced that he would be teaching an adult confirmation class, since it ends up that there were a lot of people like me who loved St. Paul's and didn't know a single thing about Lutheranism. He said that there would be information available in the narthex. I leaned over to Matthew and whispered, "The Narthex? Isn't that a Dr. Seuss character that speaks for the trees??"

"It's a lobby," he smirked. "And just the fact that you just said that makes me think maybe you should go to the class."

It was disorienting to soon find myself voluntarily spending my Wednesday nights in the basement of a church that was filled with churchgoers and not recovering alcoholics. The first day of class, "grace" was written on the chalkboard in the classroom. Pastor Ross is old school; no dry erase for him. To this day, the man types all his sermons on a typewriter. He has no computer. When I came to St. Paul's because I liked the idea that their pastor was gay, I had no idea he would end up being so old-fashioned.

He pointed to the word "grace" on the board. "Everything I'm going to tell you goes back to this," he claimed. I simultaneously doubted and hoped that was true. Most of what I had been taught by Christian clergy was that I was created by God, but was bad because of something some chick did in the Garden of Eden, and that I should try really hard to be good so that God, who is an angry bastard, won't punish me. Grace had nothing to do with it.

I hadn't learned about grace from the church. But I did learn about it from sober drunks who managed to stop drinking by giving their will over to the care of God and who then tried like hell to live a life according to spiritual principles. What the drunks taught me was that there was a power greater than myself who could be a source of restoration, and that higher power, it ends up, is not me.

A lot had happened to me in church basements. I'd had my first kiss, had been taught to fear an angry God, learned to trust a higher power, and now had my life changed again. In short, here's what Pastor Ross taught me:

- God's grace is a gift that is freely given to us. We don't earn a thing when it comes to God's love, and we only try to live in response to the gift.
- No one is climbing the spiritual ladder. We don't continually improve until we are so spiritual we no longer need God. We die and are made new, but that's different from spiritual self-improvement.
- We are simultaneously sinner and saint, 100 percent of both, all the time.
- The Bible is not God. The Bible is simply the cradle that holds Christ. Anything in the Bible that does not hold up to the Gospel of Jesus Christ simply does not have the same authority.
- The movement in our relationship to God is always from God to us. Always. We can't, through our piety or goodness, move closer to God. God is always coming near to us. Most especially in the Eucharist and in the stranger.

(Write out these bullet points, memorize them, and you could save a lot of money not going to Lutheran seminary.)

I have been a Lutheran since then because the Lutheran church is the only place that has given me language for what I have experienced to be true in my life, which is why I now call Pastor Ross Merkle the Vampire Who Turned Me.

I need to clarify something, however. God's grace is not defined as God being forgiving to us even though we sin. Grace is when God is a source of wholeness, which makes up for my failings. My failings hurt me and others and even the planet, and God's grace to me is that my brokenness is not the final word. My selfishness is not the end-all…instead, it's that God makes beautiful things out of even my own shit. Grace isn't about God creating humans as flawed beings and then acting all hurt when we inevitably fail and then stepping in like the hero to grant us grace—like saying "Oh, it's OK, I'll be a good guy and forgive you." It's God saying, "I love the world too much to let your sin define you and be the final word. I am a God who makes all things new."

So, soon after having been bitten by the Lutheran vampire, my Lutheran unicorn fiancé and I invited another couple from his seminary over for dinner and were talking about how I was loving St. Paul's and Pastor Ross and learning about Lutheran theology from such a great guy. I served them up another helping of cheese enchiladas and we laughed about Ross's inability to use email.

"What does his partner, Bob, do?" I asked.

In unison, all three replied, "Schoolteacher!" and laughed. It's a well-known stereotype that pastor's wives are always schoolteachers.

"He's such a traditional, orthodox Lutheran pastor," AmyJo offered, "which is why it was such bullshit what happened to him."

They informed me that two years earlier, Ross had been brought up on charges and endured an ecclesial trial, the result of which was his being removed from the official clergy roster of the ELCA, the Evangelical Lutheran Church in America (although his congregation chose to ignore this and continued to employ him as their pastor). Ross had not embezzled money or had an affair with his secretary. Ross's infraction was that he was in a lifelong, committed, monogamous partnership with Bob the schoolteacher. At the time, the official policy of the ELCA stated that ordained clergy were expected to be celibate in their singleness or faithful in their marriage. Ross and Bob could not be legally married, therefore Ross was in violation.

"Are you serious?" I asked. I looked at them all, waiting for a defense that would matter. "I thought I had left that kind of crap behind with altar calls and misogyny." For the rest of the night I fumed like a betrayed eighth grader.

The confirmation classes I had taken, Ross Merkle's gracious acceptance of me, and my hearing the Gospel and receiving the Eucharist at St. Paul's all felt like God again came down, tapped me on the shoulder, and said, "Pay attention, this is for you." It felt like the kingdom of heaven, and I had fallen in love with the whole Lutheran thing. But now suddenly it felt like those five minutes of a movie where the couple is gloriously ignorant of each other's shortcomings and are vapidly skipping hand-in-hand through a field of wildflowers. You know as the viewer that as soon as the montage ends, some kind of awful is going to happen. The Lutheran church was so different from the conservative Christianity of my youth and I was happy, and then the damned montage ended and I had to put the Lutherans in the same category as the Church of Christ. The one labeled "bad."

"It feels like the rug of the hope that the church might

actually be something beautiful and redemptive was pulled out from under me," I told Pastor Ross during a meeting in his office. I expected some kind of shared outrage from him. But in his humble wisdom, Pastor Ross suggested to me that God is still at work redeeming us and making all things new even in the midst of broken people and broken systems and that, despite any idealism otherwise, it had always been that way. He believed so much in the grace that the Lutheran church taught that he refused to let the failings of that same church sell their own teachings short. I found that inspiring and impossible, so I didn't reject the ELCA. But I was still angry.

"There's not enough wrong with it to leave and there's just enough wrong with it to stay," Matthew later told me. "Fight to change it."

Thirteen years later, after I had married Matthew, had two children, gone to college, gone to seminary, gotten ordained, and started a church, House for All Sinners and Saints, I sat on my bed and watched a video stream of the 2009 church-wide assembly of the ELCA (the denomination's legislative body) as they prayerfully voted to change their policy around sexual orientation. Congregations who chose to could now call as their pastor a clergyperson in a lifelong, committed, same-sex relationship.

I immediately called my parishioner Stuart who had become a leader at church soon after arriving with his boyfriend, Jim. "Thanks, ELCA!" He yelled in his most drag-queeny voice, and I cracked up.

Thanks, ELCA! was an inside joke at our church. House for All Sinners and Saints had quickly become well known in the Lutheran world, both by those who loved us and those who hated us. Those who loved us were inspired by our liturgical creativity and freedom, and those who hated us were offended by my gender (thus the term "pastrix") and by our love of the gays. And both groups liked to blog about it all. I had recently shared with my parishioners one such blog post in which someone had written: *"I can't believe the ELCA would waste money on this 'church.' Their openness to homosexuality shows that House for All Sinners and Saints has obviously thrown the Bible out the window."*

"We should totally stage a photo of HFASS with money raining down and a big sign that says 'Thanks, ELCA!'" I had said in response to the blog post.

Stuart, who was not named the House for All Sinners and Saints' Minister of Fabulousness for nothing, went a gay step further. "No," he insisted. "Everyone should be dancing and holding flutes of champagne while Pastor Nadia throws a Bible out the window and money rains down from the ceiling as a buff male dancer in a gold lamé Speedo holds a sign that says, 'Thanks, ELCA!'" And another inside joke was born.

Many of the folks at House for All had been hurt by the church in one way or another. Several, like Stuart himself, had been victims of so-called ex-gay reparative therapy at the hands of Christians, some had been told they were not up to snuff in the eyes of God, and, needless to say, the vast majority of the folks at House for All were not regularly attending a church when they joined us. In other words, they were just like me in the spring of 1996 when I first walked into St. Paul's in Oakland.

It was important to me that the House for All Sinners and Saints be a place where no one had to check at the door their personalities or the parts of our stories that seemed "unchristian." I wanted a place where something other than how we responded to rules was at the center of our life together. Yet, in the end, despite how much I love HFASS, I am still not an idealist, not when it comes to our human projects. Every human community will disappoint us, regardless of how well-intentioned or inclusive. But I *am* totally idealistic about God's redeeming work in my life and in the world.

As a matter of fact, at our quarterly "Welcome to HFASS" events, we ask the question, *What drew you to HFASS*? They love the singing, people often say, and the community, and the lack of praise bands, and the fact that they feel like they can comfortably be themselves. They love that we laugh a lot and have drag queens and that it's a place where difficult truths can be spoken and everyone is welcome, and where we pray for each other.

I am always the last to speak at these events. I tell them that I love hearing all of that and that I, too, love being in a spiritual community where I don't have to add to or take away from my own story to be accepted. But I have learned something by belonging to two polar-opposite communities—Albion Babylon and the Church of Christ—and I wanted them to hear me: This community will disappoint them. It's a matter of when, not if. We will let them down or I'll say something stupid and hurt their feelings. I then invite them on this side of their inevitable disappointment to decide if they'll stick around after it happens. If they choose to leave when we don't meet their expectations, they won't get to see how the grace of God can come in and fill the holes left by our community's failure, and that's just too beautiful and too real to miss.

Welcome to House for All Sinners and Saints. We will disappoint you.

A few months after the ELCA policy change, an email from the Lutheran bishop in Northern California arrived in my inbox.

Pastor Nadia,

We are currently planning a festival Eucharist and rite of recognition here in San Francisco for six GLBTQ [gay, lesbian, bisexual, transgender, and queer] clergy to be officially brought onto the ELCA clergy roster. At that time, Pastor Ross Merkle of St. Paul Lutheran will be reinstated onto the clergy roster. They have asked that you be the preacher for the event. Would you preach for us?

My reply: "All day long."

But then they sent me the text from which I was to preach, and my heart sank. It was a Kingdom of God parable from Matthew's Gospel. The Kingdom of God is a tricky concept, and I was always taught it referred to our heavenly reward for being good, which, now that I actually read the Bible for myself, makes very little sense. Others say that the Kingdom of God is another way of talking about the church, and still others say that it's the dream God has for the wholeness of the world, a dream being made true little by little among us right here, right now. My answer? All of the above.

What happens in the Kingdom of God parable I was given is that a landowner goes out and hires laborers in the morning and agrees to pay them the daily wage. But then every few hours he goes and finds more workers and brings them in. In the afternoon he goes again to the marketplace and sees folks standing around and is like, "Why aren't you working?" and they say, "because no one would hire us," and he sends them into his vineyard to work the last two hours of the day. When the work is done he pays everyone the same thing, which pisses off the upstanding early risers who worked all day in the scorching heat because he has made the slept-till-noon new hires equal to them. The land-owner is like, "Seriously? You're angry because I am generous?" and then the final line of the parable is, "The last shall be first and the first shall be last." This is exactly, when it comes down to it, why most people do not believe in grace. It is fucking offensive.

But the job of a preacher is to find some kind of good news for people. And that good news really should be about who God is and how God works and what God has done and what God will do. (What passes for preaching in many cases is more *here's the problem, and here's what you can do about it*, which I myself have never once heard as being "good news.") So here's why my heart sank when I received the text for the Eucharist: I worried that it might have been chosen in the hope that I would preach a different kind of good news, namely a sermon that said, "All those who are pissed that God is generous to GLBTQ folks can suck it. We've been last, but now we get to be first! [fist pump]"

Yet that's the problem with the whole concept of grace that the Lutherans themselves taught me. It can both sting and comfort. My own fundamentalist wiring will always lead me to want two sets of labeled containers—in this case, Bad: the conservative people who hate the gays and Good: the liberal people who love the gays. I might always put people and things in those containers, but the problem comes when I start believing that God uses the same sorting system.

Matthew once said to me, after one of my more finely worded rants about stupid people who have the wrong opinions, "Nadia, the thing that sucks is that every time we draw a line between us and others, Jesus is always on the other side of it." Damn.

I want the kingdom of God, and myself, and the ELCA, to be more impressive, more...spiritual. To look like I think it should. But I have learned that like this parable the kingdom of God is more like a workplace—filled with type A personalities, whose sense of entitlement would rival Paris Hilton's, alongside slackers, who take too many smoke breaks and spend their money on scratch tickets.

But here's one of the things that sealed the deal for me with Lutheranism and set the tone for the kind of pastor I would try to be: What makes this the kingdom of God is not the quality of the people in it. What makes Lutherans blessed is not, as I once thought, that they're somehow different from the people in the Church of Christ where I was raised. Rather, what makes us *all* blessed is that, like the landowner in the parable, God comes and gets us, taps us on the shoulder, and says "Pay attention, this is for you." Dumb as we are, smart and faithful as we are, just as we are. Which is just what I preached that day.

As I stood in the imposing pulpit of St. Mark's Lutheran

church in San Francisco, I looked out into the faces of those who had been unfairly denied entrance into the leadership of the church. I looked out into the faces of Stuart and Jim, who had come from Denver to witness the celebration (and who, moments earlier, when standing outside with over a hundred clergy ready to process in full vestments, had looked at me and laughed, saying, "This looks like such a big deal, and you're the preacher?"). I looked at sweet Ross Merkle who winked at me.

I swallowed and began to preach. I said that the text for the day is not the parable of the workers. It's the parable of the landowner. What makes this the kingdom of God is not the worthiness or piety or social justicey-ness or the hard work of the laborers...none of that matters. It's the fact that the trampy landowner couldn't manage to keep out of the marketplace. He goes back and back and back, interrupting lives... coming to get his people. Grace tapping us on the shoulder.

And so, I reminded those seven pastors specifically, including the man who introduced me to grace, that the kingdom of God was just like that exact moment in which sinners/saints are reconciled to God and to one another. The kingdom of God is like that very moment when God was making all things new. In the end, their calling, and their value in the kingdom of God comes not from the approval of a denomination or of the other workers, but in their having been come-and-gotten by God. It is the pure and unfathomable mercy of God that defines them and that says, "Pay attention, this is for you."

CHAPTER 6

Hurricanes and Humiliation

How does God's love abide in anyone who has the world's goods and sees a brother or sister in need and yet refuses help?

Little children, let us love, not in word or speech, but in truth and action.

—1 John 3:17-18

Driving back from Lowry Air Force Base on a fall day in 2005 (when I was just starting seminary and our kids, Harper and Judah, were five and seven), I was giddy with self-congratulations. I had rescued a pregnant, disadvantaged, teenaged African American girl (and her father)—victims of a natural disaster—and I was about to give them a new life. This was a white privileged liberal's dream, and I was riding high on it, when suddenly a *thunk* the likes of which no car owner ever wants to hear, came out of my Honda like a bitch slap.

The interior of the car became suspiciously warmer and warmer until I could no longer deny that my air conditioner had just broken. If I believed in portents, which I do, but only in retrospect and never as something to heed in the moment (which basically neuters their usefulness as portents), I would have perhaps taken notice—sort of like that tiki from the *Brady Bunch* episode in Hawaii, but I generally ignore my personal tikis until well into syndication.

We were driving away from the decommissioned air force base outside of Denver where many Hurricane Katrina evacuees were being housed. Earlier that week, I, like the rest of America, had watched in horror as images of death and disaster had been splashed across our TV screens, and this time they were domestic. We got the smallest glimpse of what most of the world suffers on a daily basis and we were scandalized. Folks from my husband Matthew's congregation had been calling us all week with offers of assistance—free housing, kitchen supplies, clothing, money, and employment for the evacuees—but no one could figure out how to get these resources to those who needed them. That our only option was to list our offers of help on a national Web site and just wait seemed silly to me. People were being evacuated to our own area who could use these things right now, not three months from now when some bureaucrat finally connects the dots. I was going to take care of this now.

I, like others, could not abide the images of people stranded on rooftops, of lifeless bodies floating in debris-filled water or covered with sheets in the hallway of a purgatorial sports coliseum.

If I could help a family set up a new life here in Colorado, then I could exonerate myself from the charges leveled by these images and right a wrong at the same time. In light of our government's anemic response, I wanted to heroically rescue a victim from this unthinkable disaster.

I went looking for the perfect family; a single man wouldn't do. When I saw Amerie, I knew she was the one: a sixteen-year-old from New Orleans who was almost eight months pregnant. We met at the air force barracks where she was in line to ask the Red Cross volunteers if they could find her a place to live that wasn't...in a barracks. They couldn't, but [insert superhero sound here] I could.

Soft spoken and polite with coffee ice cream skin, Amerie was interested in what I had to offer: a fully furnished apartment, rent free for six months, with money for groceries and expenses (after a single announcement at Matthew's church a few days earlier, I collected a cool two thousand dollars in cash). Her dad was with her, and I assured her that the offer extended to him as well. Later that afternoon she called me and said they'd take it. I picked up them and their two Hefty bags full of stuff, and the three of us drove silently toward my house in a blistering hot Honda. The high of the rescue then wore off, and I was left with a blank feeling of slight dread, like Dustin Hoffman and Katharine Ross riding away on a city bus in the last scene of *The Graduate*.

Amerie's mother was a drug addict who had been MIA for the last four months, so her father, Howard, a dark-skinned man of few words, had come from the Bronx to look after her. Her parents had never married, but Amerie explained that Howard had always kept in touch, sending money when he could, which had been difficult during his time as a guest of the state of New York after being convicted of being a "street pharmacist."

Howard had only been in New Orleans for a month when the hurricane hit. "She was dumb enough to get herself in this condition, so I should have just left her," he said to me, waving his hand in the direction of his pregnant daughter, who sat in the blazing hot backseat of my car. They had made it to Houston before their car broke down, and from there, a friend drove them to Denver.

For the next six weeks, I, along with two other women from church, took care of Amerie. We got her into birthing classes and a teen parenting program in a Boulder high school and made appointments with a great ob-gyn at the hospital. She often stayed at our house. Howard had a job in Denver and almost always stayed at the barracks.

Amerie was wonderful with my kids. She spent hours playing board games and sitting contentedly petting the cat. But I worried about how she was left alone so often by her father this close to her due date and without a car of her own. She never talked much about her previous life except to say that she wanted something different from drug addiction and public housing. She wanted to stay in Colorado.

But there were things that didn't quite add up. Amerie never tried to contact her mother. Her father was mostly absent, and when he was around he was completely unkind to her. They had four thousand dollars from FEMA and a free apartment and lots of grocery store gift cards, but still kept asking every few days for more money. And unlike most teenagers, the urgent way Amerie always reacted when she got a text seemed more like she had just received a telegram during wartime than a frivolous exchange between locker partners. But whenever I started questioning the situation, I told myself that I just didn't understand black poverty culture.

Howard soon had a girlfriend near the barracks, and when we met, she made me uncomfortable. She smelled of menthol cigarettes, was a decade too old for a bleach-blond ponytail, and the ten-year-old son by her side never seemed to be in school. To my eyes this woman was totally unstable, and why Amerie would want to be around her was beyond me. But she apparently liked the woman, and I couldn't stop that.

Amerie went into labor on the first day of Advent. It seemed perfect that this unwed, homeless teenager was having this baby at the beginning of the season in which the church remembers another homeless, unwed teenage mother. She was so brave in labor, refusing drugs and filling the room with such calm and strength as she faced each contraction.

Two church ladies, the childbirth instructor, and Howard's girlfriend (with her ten-year-old, of course) were all there, but Howard, I was told, "was out drinking somewhere." After hours of labor, Amerie wasn't progressing, so everyone but me went home, having been told that nothing would be happening until at least the morning. A couple of hours later, Amerie was advised to consider an epidural, which she welcomed.

But relief from the pain soon gave way to panic. The epidural had not gone well. Within ten minutes the baby's heart rate had dropped to dangerous levels, and a set of scrubs was being thrust in my face as we were rushed into the bright noise and uncertainly of an operating room. I kept caressing Amerie's face and telling her that I was right there and she was going to be fine, something Matthew had done for me in both of my labors. The fetal monitor provided a cruel soundtrack to the chaos around us, like an uneven and slowing time clock. It felt like it took the doctors and nurses a lifetime to complete the C-section. Finally they pulled a beautiful screaming child out of the body of a beautiful screaming child, and they were both fine. Amerie and I both wept in that moment of new life that marks the souls of those who share it. We'd take care of her and her baby. Even if her dad couldn't, we'd make sure this little girl had a good life. The first question she asked when the baby was born was, "Is she OK?" The second question she asked was, "Is she dark?"

Amerie and her baby girl came and stayed a couple of nights with us before she planned (much to my dismay) to stay with her father's girlfriend for a while. She left on a Thursday. That same night, as I was about to go to bed, the phone rang. Amerie was hysterical for the first time since I'd known her.

"We're in trouble. You have to meet us," she said. I panicked, sure something had happened with the baby. She assured me the baby was fine and that she had to speak to me in person. I had to help her, she said. Suddenly I wasn't the helpful Nellie I'd been until then, and all I could think was, *are you kidding me? I've done nothing but help you for a month and a half. I'm exhausted, and if I don't sleep soon I'm going to become subhuman.* Instead I said, "I'll be there, just hold on." We got a neighbor to come over and babysit the kids, and then Matthew drove us to an exit off the highway where Amerie had said they'd be waiting for us.

It was raining when Amerie and Howard's girlfriend climbed into the backseat with the baby. Amerie was crying, but the baby was quiet.

"We're in trouble," she said again. "You have to help us."

She proceeded to tell me that her name is not Amerie, but Ashley. Howard is not her father, but the father of the baby. This is not Howard's girlfriend; she's Amerie's mother. Howard is her mother's pimp, and he raped Amerie. She is not sixteen; she's only fifteen, meaning she was fourteen at the time of the rape. They are not even from New Orleans; they're from Denver. Howard put her up to the fraud, and he ended up with four thousand dollars in a bank account thanks to FEMA, which was his plan all along. Her phone buzzed repeatedly as she told me the story, and she jumped a little each time. Howard was texting.

"We want to get away from him," Amerie said. "I understand if you don't want to help us, but we don't know what else to do."

I hated being lied to. And my heart felt smaller and harder with every word out of her mouth. My mind was trying to remember everything from the last six weeks in a matter of seconds in order to retell myself the story so that it would make sense again. What had I done? All that money Matthew's church gave. All the little comments I made in her childbirth class and while registering her for high school: She's a Katrina survivor. Which really meant, *You may have given the Red Cross twenty-five dollars, but I'm helping a real, live pregnant teenager from New Orleans.* When in actuality, I was being conned by a pimp and a prostitute from Denver.

We called the police, who got Amerie, her daughter, and her mother into a battered women's shelter.

I never saw them again.

On our way home, Matthew and I realized that the last time Howard knew where his victims were, they were at our house, and our children were there now. Speeding home, I prayed they were safe. Those rain-soaked streets on that Thursday night in January were longer than they had ever been.

Four blocks from our house, we saw the flashing lights of several police vehicles driving toward us. I fought to breathe, waiting to see if they made the turn to our house. We exhaled as they passed our street, and I cried uncontrollably. We ran into the house, grabbed the kids, and slept at my parents' house for the next three nights.

There are times when you just don't know what to feel, because you feel things that don't normally mix in polite company. I felt angry and ashamed at having been conned. I felt deep sorrow for a sweet child and her baby who were victims of a situation far sadder than a hurricane. I felt disappointment in myself for not really wanting to help her anymore. But I hated being lied to. I hate being lied to.

The next Sunday, I was ashamed to face Matthew's congregation, who had been told the truth of the Amerie situation in an email the day before. I could just see them coldly avoiding me or, worse, telling me not to "feel bad." Walking in I tried to not make eye contact with anyone, but an older woman who I hadn't really interacted with much in the past walked up to me in her piously pink dress and heels. I braced myself.

"Nadia," she said, with a kindness I'll not soon forget, "God was still glorified in this. Who knows if Amerie would ever have had the courage to leave him if she hadn't received the love she had over the past month while part of our community. Maybe now they know that they are worth more than the life they've always had."

I cried.

I often feel like God uses other people to tell us stuff we need to know, and on that Sunday I needed to know that I hadn't failed, but had been doing a kind of work of which I wasn't even aware. Still, of all the betrayals in that circumstance, it was my betrayal of myself that stung the most. So much about the situation didn't add up. Those little security analysts in my head had been trying to tell me that something wasn't right, and I refused to listen. I even went so far as to put my children in harm's way, just so I could play the hero. I've not completely forgiven myself for that, but I'm trying.

Jesus calls us to welcome the stranger and serve our neighbor. And the images on our television during the Katrina event begged the question: Who is that neighbor? Being Christian is much harder than I wish it was. We're called to take care of the poor. But should we open our homes to those in need if it entails danger to our children? We're called to love our enemies and forgive those who trespass against us. Does that mean we should allow people who have hurt and betrayed us back into our lives? Or does it mean that we simply don't wish them ill? I really loved Amerie, but do I love Ashley? I'm haunted by how much of my love was based on my need to be seen as heroic, and yet I can't deny that it did feel like love.

A better Christian would love her anyway and still want to help her. A lousy Christian is conflicted and maybe a little hurt. She wishes Ashley well, but doesn't want her to show up at the front door anytime soon. I'm a lousy Christian, and I hope that's good enough since our call to be compassionate has to include ourselves, too.

In the days that followed, I was depressed and demoralized. I called my sister, who assured me that God uses our humiliations as much as our victories, which may have just been an act of aggression on her part; but maybe, despite that, she's right.

✣ CHAPTER 7 ✣

I Didn't Call You for This
Truth Bullshit

And this is the judgment, that the light has come into the world, and people loved darkness rather than light because their deeds were evil. For all who do evil hate the light and do not come to the light, so that their deeds may not be exposed. But those who do what is true come to the light, so that it may be clearly seen that their deeds have been done in God.

—*John 3: 19-21*

Our house has two sinks for some reason," Candace said as she filled a bowl with cereal for me. "It has something to do with being Jewish, or something."

She was right, of course, having two sinks does have something to do with being Jewish. A kosher kitchen has two sinks and often two refrigerators and two dishwashers, or at least one with changeable racks, so that what touches meat does not touch dairy. It was weird having all this (mostly useless) religious knowledge thanks to my new seminary education. I know almost nothing about sports or politics, but I can tell you why my friend Candace now has two sinks.

She and her husband bought the house, a modern, poshly renovated three-story two months before, because when attempting an open marriage doesn't save a relationship, then perhaps a half-million-dollar mortgage can do the trick. Except in their case, when it didn't.

Candace didn't know a lot about kitchens because Candace grew up in New England, in a house that had a staff. Most of her life she'd been able to buy what she lacked, unless it was emotional. She's ginger haired and voluptuous, and favored tight T-shirts and short skirts. As she put it, her debutante ball was more than she could handle, so it's a good thing she was high on heroin at the time.

We met in an alcohol recovery meeting a few years earlier and became friends based purely on the unlikely number of things we had in common. We both had colorful pasts but were clean now. We both had collected a long string of damaged boyfriends and girlfriends, some of whom were convicted felons, but we had both gotten married to nice men, had a couple of kids, and had managed to go back to both church and school. We leaned on each other because it's hard keeping so many contradictions together by yourself. And when your life has changed so much in ten years, sometimes the memory of who you were emerges from the milky mist of your consciousness and starts whispering,

"Remember me?" And when that happens, you just have to have a girlfriend around who gets it because if you ignore the whispers they become screams, and then you just can't shut the bitch up.

"Jesus, Nadia," she said as I scarfed the cereal, "is that your dinner?" I'd just arrived from my Hebrew Bible study group after a full day of seminary classes and hadn't yet stopped to eat when Candace had called and said she needed me.

Being a loyal friend is something I haven't always been good at, so at the time, I was trying to make up for my past disloyalties by being (or just making it look like I was) selfless. Candace's marriage was now ending badly, and she could only have her daughters overnight if someone was there with her. She was an ex-junkie with medical complaints, real or imagined, who had found some idiot doctor to prescribe her Oxy-Contin. Her justifications for using it were both endless and creative: Her medical conditions caused her so much pain that she needed the drug to even function; she didn't really want to take the pain meds but her doctor insisted; really her pain was so great she wasn't even able to get high off the Oxy. Her marriage was ending and I was trying to support her.

At the time I was also trying futilely to believe she was still clean and sober. I was supposedly one of the only people she could get to be with her for overnight visits with her kids. So while I was commuting an hour each way to seminary and had small children of my own, I was also showing up for her when I could, even if it meant eating cereal for dinner.

We'd been doing this for a few weeks: me trying to do what I thought a loyal friend would do, her seeming to do whatever she could to keep the Oxy in her system. Me stretching my time and life too thin, her getting twice the sleep I was. We were like twins in utero, one taking all the nutrients, and the other becoming scrawny as a result.

I eventually tried, just once, to confront her about what I was convinced was the truth: She was addicted again. But unlike almost every other situation in my life, I had lost my boldness. As soon as she gave me the *I'm in crisis and need you to support me* look, I backed off. That look was too similar to one I had justly deserved in my past friendships. I would be as "loyal" to Candace as it took to avoid that look and maybe make up for not sticking with Amerie/Ashley.

One morning, when driving home from Candace's house, I called my older sister and told her how tired I was and also how much my friend needed me. Barbara had always been naturally interested in helping others, and I knew she would be proud of me.

"Nadia," she said, "you have a limited amount of time and emotional energy in your life, and you are squandering tons of it on this one situation just so you can maintain the idea you like to have of yourself as being a loyal friend."

"Look," I said, in my own defense, "I didn't call you for this truth bullshit." (The late writer David Foster Wallace was right: The truth *will* set you free...but not before it's done with you.)

Years later, after I had started House for All Sinners and Saints, I thought of Candace when I was writing a sermon about when Jesus goes on and on about how we really actually like darkness more than light because, let's face it, the darkness hides our bullshit. (Revised Nadia Version.) I thought of all the time I spent trying to be good and all the time she spent trying to pretend she wasn't high and how perfectly matched our crap was. And all it took was my sister speaking the truth about it for light to come and scatter the darkness. I thought about how, just like Candace, when I want desperately for something about myself to be hidden, for it to stay in the darkness, I am really good at lying. And if I can go an extra step and make it look like I'm actually being good—if I can pawn off narcissism as a virtue—then I win. Like when I am just sick of giving a shit about other people and want to be selfish so I call my two days of watching Netflix and getting mani-pedis "self-care." Or when I say I'm on "a cleanse" so no one knows I'm really on a diet.

The list goes on, and the last thing I want is for any light to be cast on the darkness that I've spent so much energy curating, protecting, enjoying. But it's not a cleanse. It's a diet. It's not about my health, it's about my vanity.

There's a popular misconception that religion, Christianity specifically, is about knowing the difference between good and evil so that we can choose the good. But being good has never set me free the way truth has. Knowing all of this makes me love and hate Jesus at the same time. Because, when instead of contrasting good and evil, he contrasted truth and evil, I have to think about all the times I've substituted being good (or appearing to be good) for truth.

Very often I will avoid the truth until my face goes red like a toddler avoiding her nap; until limp limbed, she finally stops flailing and falls asleep and receives rest—the very thing she needs and the very thing she fights. When someone like me, who will go to superhero lengths to avoid the truth, runs out of options—when I am found out or too exhausted to pretend anymore or maybe just confronted by my sister—it feels like the truth might crush me. And that is right. The truth does crush us, but the instant it crushes us, it somehow puts us back together into something honest. It's death and resurrection every time it happens.

This, to me, is the point of the confession and absolution in the liturgy. When I first experienced it—the part where everyone in church stands up and says what bad people they are, and the pastor, from the distance of the chancel and the purity of her white robe says, "God forgives you"—I thought it was hogwash. Why should I care if someone says to me that some God I may or may not really believe in has erased the check marks against me for things I may or may not even think are so-called sins? This obviously is the problem with religion for so many: It makes you feel bad enough that you will need the religion to help you feel good again.

But eventually the confession and absolution liturgy came to mean everything to me. It gradually began to feel like a moment when truth was spoken, perhaps for the only time all week, and it would crush me and then put me back together.

One Sunday in 2006, after the last night I spent at Candace's house, I stood in the blue-carpeted sanctuary at my husband's church and for the first time I really paid attention to the confession.

We have sinned by what we have done and by what we have left undone. We have not loved you with our whole heart. We have not loved our neighbors as ourselves.

Saying the words that morning with all the elderly transplanted Minnesotans, young mothers, and distracted teenagers, I felt like I had just said the truth about myself (the specifics about Candace and my pretending didn't matter), and it felt like that feeling I'd get in the backseat of my parents' car when I finally exhaled after holding my breath through a mountain tunnel.

And then the pastor said, "Fear not, brothers and sisters, God, who is full of grace and abounding in steadfast love, meets us in our sin and transforms us for God's glory and the healing of God's world. In the name of the Father, the Son, and the Holy Spirit, your sins are forgiven, be now at peace."

Exhale.

✠

In 2009, a year after I had started House for All Sinners and Saints, Candace emailed asking if she could come to church. I said yes, but that we should meet first.

Later we would walk through the city park, passing moms and their sticky-faced toddlers and the homeless men napping under trees like urban Monet paintings, geese gliding in the lake behind them. She and I had shown up wearing almost identical black T-shirts with flowers, low cut. It was good to see her, and I longed for the friendship I knew was gone—for the times when we had the same story and it was effortless to be together. At one point we matched, she and I. Now it was just the T-shirts. I had aged in the years since I stopped saying yes to her. I had a couple extra wrinkles and sags. But not her. Her forehead didn't move when she talked, and her mouth had enough crap injected into it that the protruding upper portion had begun to resemble a bill rather than a lip. There wasn't much truth to her.

As we walked, she told me of the divorce and her health and all the reasons she just can't work a job: fibromyalgia, chronic fatigue syndrome. Things that often come with soft diagnoses and hard prescriptions. I thought back to when my children, Harper and Judah, were young and I was unhappy and had come down with a wee touch of hypochondria. The demands of staying at home with a baby and a toddler were too much, and I got sick a lot, which convinced me that something was really wrong with me. I wanted something to be wrong with me. I wanted a hall pass for a while so no one would expect anything of me. But the tests always came back negative and, finally, after my third visit to the doctor in two months, he said, "Nadia, nothing's wrong with you. You just have to deal with your life." Truth. It can make me hate the person speaking it. Until the point at which I want to kiss them for setting me free.

But I still couldn't be that person for Candace. She said she wanted to be a part of the church and also to be my friend again, for us to lean on each other. I was torn between "being good"—saying yes, by all means, come and be my friend and parishioner, someone like you could really use a nice church—and wanting to tell the truth and say I just cannot trust her and as a Lutheran clergywoman I need people a touch more stable to lean on. But I couldn't. Something about us matching each other in the past, no matter how much we no longer matched in the present, made me feel as though I had no right.

I wish I could say that I had learned how powerful the truth is and that I am unwavering in my commitment to it. But in that moment I couldn't manage to be good *or* tell the truth. Instead, I said that I had the friends I needed. Sometimes we can't manage to choose the truth or to be good, and in those moments I just hope God comes and does that thing where something is transformed into healing anyway.

Candace came to church once. She kind of laughed as I served her communion and then never came back.

✠ CHAPTER 8 ✠

Clinical Pastoral Education

When they came to the place that is called The Skull, they crucified Jesus there with the criminals, one on his right and one
on his left.

—*Luke 23:33*

It was 2007 and I was clunking along nicely in seminary,
writing papers, triaging the inordinate amount of reading,
and usually showing up for class, when I realized there was a
requirement that I had somehow missed: clinical pastoral education. You want to be a pastor? Great. But first you have to
work for ten weeks as a hospital chaplain. This felt to me like
saying "You want to be a cab driver? Great. But first, here are
the keys to an ambulance, they are yours for the next two-
and-a-half months."

This is what was required of me to become a student chaplain at a hospital: I filled out a CPE application, and then they handed me a clipboard and a name badge. Voilà! I am now a hospital chaplain. I felt about as qualified to wear the chaplain's badge as I did to don scrubs and a stethoscope.

When I knocked on the dusty–rose colored door of my first patient and said, "Hi, I'm Nadia, from the chaplain's office," I was sure the patient would immediately know two things: (1) I'm not really a hospital chaplain and (2) I had just bought the clothes I'm wearing the day before. At thirty-seven I had, for the first time in my life, a need to own grown-up drag: slacks, blazers, and shirts that not only buttoned, but also covered my heavily tattooed arms. Yet dressing like an adult didn't make me feel more confident; it made me feel even more like a fraud.

That first day, I walked around the surgical unit trying to figure out what the hell I was supposed to be doing. "Is there anything the chaplain's office can do for you?" I asked an elderly woman recovering from shoulder surgery, expecting her to ask me to pray or bring her a Bible. Or possibly she had a prayer book covered in pictures of angels hidden in the drawer and from which I could read to her. "Oh that's all nonsense, dear. I'm an atheist." Before realizing I was saying it, I blurted out admiringly, "Man, good for you. I wish I could pull that off."

During my next visit, to another elderly orthopedic patient, I again struggled to figure out what I was supposed to say, so instead I sat in the cheerful waterproof chair and watched Court TV with him. I had forgotten I was wearing a pager until it started buzzing, causing me to miss the Court TV ruling. It was the ER.

There were a couple things I didn't know that just moments before had not been an issue for me: Would Tyra get her cleaning deposit back from her pockmarked landlord? And where is the ER?

"I was paged?" I said to the security guard at the ER desk. She offered me a sarcastic "congratulations" look and went back to her crossword.

"Uh, I'm from the chaplain's office?" I said. She pointed to a door that said NO ADMITTANCE and then looked at me like I was an idiot. Apparently my name badge allowed me to go through doors like that.

I finally found a nurse who would make eye contact with me. I said I was paged, but that I wasn't sure what for.

"Trauma one," she said.

Inside the trauma room, a nurse was cutting the clothes off a motionless man in his fifties on a table; tubes were coming out of his mouth and arms. Doctors started doing things to him not meant for my eyes and sorely misrepresented on TV shows. Another nurse was hooking things up to him while a doctor put on gloves and motioned for paddles, which he then placed into the motionless man's freshly cracked-open chest.

A nurse stepped back to where I was standing, and I leaned over to her. "Everyone seems to have a job, but what am I doing here?"

She looked at my badge and said, "Your job is to be aware of God's presence in the room while we do our jobs."

For the rest of those two-and-a-half months I often found myself in the ER trauma room watching life going in and out of the patients on the table—the doctors and nurses violently attempting to resuscitate them. And in that messy chaos, my job was to just stand there and be aware of God's presence in the room. Kind of a weird job description, but there it was, and in those moments, I felt strangely qualified. I didn't have the slightest idea what to say to someone who just had shoulder surgery, but I couldn't help but feel God's presence in the trauma room.

It wasn't long before I found myself sensing God's presence in other rooms, too. I felt it in the little white room with just enough space for four love seats and as many boxes of tissue where we brought the families of those who are dead, or might be dead, or should be dead, or had died and are now not dead, but we don't know for how long. I'd sit with people in their loss. Their sixty-year-old father has just died. Their spouse of thirty-one years has just experienced a brain aneurism. Their sister has just swallowed four bottles of pills and they are waiting to hear if her body is dead or just her brain. In this little white pit of pain, I was the chaplain.

I noticed that the family and friends of those who had unexpectedly died, in a grief so thick it sucked the oxygen out of the room, would gaze off and say, "Just this morning we were eating breakfast and talking about baseball," or "We were just walking the dog, laughing about the kids."

The life changing seems always bracketed by the mundane. The quotidian wrapped around the profound, like plain brown paper concealing the emotional version of an improvised explosive devise. Then, in a single interminable moment, when we discover the bomb, absolutely everything changes. But when we recall it from our now forever–changed lives, when we start with the plain brown wrapping, it looks like every other package, every other morning, every other walk.

The Tuesday of Holy Week, I was sitting in the windowless chaplain's office filling in my paperwork when the ER paged me. I had just remembered that my kids' Easter baskets would be empty on Sunday if I didn't remember to stop by Target in the next couple days.

When I got to the ER, things felt different. Quiet.

On the table was a thirty-one-year-old DOA. She was killed when she stepped out of her car on the highway. Her two-year-old and five-year-old sons were in the minivan. "They are unhurt, and we need you to stay with them until other family can arrive," I was instructed.

They were unhurt. Right.

I took the boys hand in hand to pediatrics, where there are toys and TVs. We found some trucks to play with on the floor, and as I scooted a red fire engine back and forth over the cheerful linoleum, I was aware that for the rest of these boys' lives, this would be the day their mom died. This would be the day they sat scared and crying in a minivan until the police arrived. This would be the day that their mom was taken from them before they could really even know who she was and before she could love them into adulthood. I'm not sure what else I could have given them but juice boxes and my time. Two hours later, when their extended family showed up, I almost offered to buy their Easter baskets.

I was the chaplain, but I didn't have answers for anyone. I'd bring people water, make some calls for them, keep bugging the doctors to provide more information, but words of wisdom I had none. I just felt the unfairness of it all. I felt the uncontrollable terror of loss, the finality of someone never having a father again. I felt a sadness that is both poetic and grotesque. I would stand by and witness the disfiguring emotional process we politely call grief and, yes, I was aware of God's presence, but I wanted to slap the hell out of him or her or it.

After all, maybe if God sensed that I wasn't a girl to fuck with, then *my* loved ones would be spared. I couldn't stop thinking about my own husband and children. Harper and Judah were small at the time, and I needed them to be able to live in a world where their mom might not just die outside a minivan on a Tuesday in Holy Week. And sometimes, before I could stop myself, I'd think *what if that were Matthew on the table?* And then I'd get angry, that defensive kind of angry. The kind of angry that keeps the fear from embarrassing you. Or taking over.

You hear a lot of nonsense in hospitals and funeral homes. God had a plan, we just don't know what it is. Maybe God took your daughter because He needs another angel in heaven. But when I've experienced loss and felt so much pain that it feels like nothing else ever existed, the last thing I need is a well-meaning but vapid person saying that when God closes a door he opens a window. It makes me want to ask where exactly that window is so I can push him the fuck out of it.

But this is the nonsense spawned from bad religion. And usually when you are grieving and someone says something so senselessly optimistic to you, it's about them. Either they want to feel like they can say something helpful, or they simply cannot allow themselves to entertain the finality and pain of death, so instead they turn it into a Precious Moments greeting card. I've both had those things said to me and have been the one to say them. But as a chaplain, I felt that people really just needed me to mostly shut the hell up and deal with the reality of how painful it all is.

When I first began dipping my toe back into the waters of Christianity, back when Matthew and I were dating, I read a lot. Mostly I read Marcus Borg and others who had done work on what is called the Historical Jesus. Matthew had given me a book called *Meeting Jesus Again for the First Time*. It was my gateway drug. Unlike what I saw as the irrational faith of my fundamentalist upbringing, these people were scholarly and reasonable and searched for what we could really know about the man Jesus of Nazareth. He was a Palestinian Jew in the first century who garnered a following based on his charisma and teaching. Man, was he a great guy, really in touch with his God consciousness. I loved these people for rescuing the image of Christ from the bondage of ignorance and the religious right, and I felt high on meeting Jesus again for what really did feel like the first time.

This was the bonus to liberal Christianity: I could use my reason and believe at the same time. But it only worked for me for a short while. And soon I wanted to experiment with the harder stuff. Admiring Jesus, while a noble pursuit, doesn't show me where God is to be found when we suffer the death of a loved one or a terrifying cancer diagnosis or when our child is hurt. Admiring and trying to imitate a guy who was really in touch with God just doesn't seem to bridge the distance between me and the Almighty in ways that help me understand where the hell God is when we are suffering.

And of course I didn't get much help in childhood. The image of God I was raised with was this: God is an angry bastard with a killer surveillance system who had to send his little boy (and he only had one) to suffer and die because I was bad. But the good news was that if I believed this story and then tried really hard to be good, when I died I would go to heaven, where I would live in a golden gated community with God and all the other people who believed and did the same things as I did. (When I was estranged from my conservative Christian parents, I used to joke that my mom would say, in her slight Kentucky accent, "Nadia, the least you could do is come visit us more often, since we *won't* be spending eternity together." I wondered if my parents understood that spending eternity with them and their friends is not exactly their church's best selling point.) And anyway, this type of thinking portrays God as just as mean and selfish as we are, which feels like it has a lot more to do with our own greed and spite than it has to do with God.

The choir at Matthew's church sang that Good Friday—three days after I had sat with two small, motherless boys on a hospital floor. I sat in the back pew and listened to the beautiful

Latin and ancient melody coming from the voices of the people before me. When the reading of the passion began—the account in John's Gospel of the betrayal, suffering, and death of Jesus—I listened with changed ears. I listened with the ears of someone who didn't just admire and want to imitate Jesus, but had felt him present in the room where two motherless boys played on the floor.

I was stunned that Good Friday by this familiar but foreign story of Jesus' last hours, and I realized that in Jesus, God had come to dwell with us and share our human story. Even the parts of our human story that are the most painful. God was not sitting in heaven looking down at Jesus' life and death and cruelly allowing his son to suffer. God was not looking down on the cross. God was hanging *from* the cross. God had entered our pain and loss and death so deeply and took all of it into God's own self so that we might know who God really is. Maybe the Good Friday story is about how God would rather die than be in our sin-accounting business anymore.

The passion reading ended, and suddenly I was aware that God isn't feeling smug about the whole thing. God is not distant at the cross and God is not distant in the grief of the newly motherless at the hospital; but instead, God is there in the messy mascara-streaked middle of it, feeling as shitty as the rest of us. There simply is no knowable answer to the question of why there is suffering. But there is meaning. And for me that meaning ended up being related to Jesus—Emmanuel—which means "God with us." We want to go to God for answers, but sometimes what we get is God's presence.

✥ CHAPTER 9 ✥

Eunuchs and Hermaphrodites

As they were going along the road, they came to some water; and the eunuch said, Look, here is water! What is to prevent me from being baptized?

—Acts 8:36

The 1980s pop star Tiffany has a hermaphrodite[1] obsessive who once helped me write a sermon. Kelly, the hermaphrodite in question, doesn't know that she helped me write a sermon. All she did was walk into the same coffee shop in Denver where I was at that moment struggling to write a sermon for my fledgling new church about Philip and the Ethiopian eunuch. We Lutherans, as well as most Catholics, Presbyterians, Methodists, and Episcopalians, use the same set of assigned texts

---

1. Hermaphrodite is often seen as a derogatory term. But it is how Kelly refers to herself.

to preach from each Sunday. It's called the Revised Common Lectionary. The passage on the Ethiopian eunuch was the assigned text for that week, and although using the assigned texts is an expectation, not a law, I've just never trusted myself enough to go off reservation. The last thing my people need is for me to start deciding what verses to preach from each Sunday. I'd give it three months before that turned into a *Heart of Darkness* situation.

When I saw Kelly, I first felt shock, followed quickly by revulsion: shock because I had seen a documentary about her just two days before (*I Think We're Alone Now*—about her and another Tiffany-obsessed fan, a fifty-year-old man with Asperger's); revulsion at how both male and female she seemed. She wasn't cool androgynous like David Bowie or Annie Lennox. Kelly had long hair like a woman, a face that seemed both female and male, breasts, and a man's midsection and thick legs.

Then I experienced shame. I was ashamed of feeling repulsed. I've been around gay men and queer gals and transgender folks most of my life and yet I felt disgusted by this intersex person in front of me.

Watching documentaries about intersex celebrity obsessives usually doesn't fit neatly into my workweek, but I had been doing some research about eunuchs for a sermon, and the black hole of the Internet sucked me into watching *I Think We're Alone Now*. And then Kelly walked into the coffee shop I frequented. She was with another woman, and they both ordered drinks to go. I sat there stunned, half expecting Tina

Fey to walk in next; I had, after all, watched *30 Rock* the night before.

Fey never showed, and I still had no sermon about the eunuch from Ethiopia. I had words on paper, but they were stupid.

The story of the Ethiopian eunuch comes from the book of Acts. After Jesus had risen from the dead, messed with everyone's heads, grilled them all a fish breakfast on the beach, and had a few more choice meals, he then ascended into heaven. But not before telling his followers to tell the story about him to all peoples and baptizing them in the name of the Trinity.

The first gentile convert ended up being a black sexual minority. The story goes that the Spirit told Philip to go to this certain desert road. There he found a eunuch in a chariot who was reading from the scroll of Isaiah. Philip climbs in the chariot and tells this castrated man from Ethiopia about Jesus, at which point the eunuch says, "Look over there! There is water. What keeps me from being baptized?" Philip baptizes him and then vanishes.

Growing up I always heard this story called "The Conversion of the Ethiopian Eunuch." I was always told that the message of this text was that we should tell everyone we meet about Jesus because in doing so we might save them. We might convert them. We might change them into being us so they, too, can live in a mansion in heaven, but of course probably not one as nice as ours. But reading it now I found that it's all such great material for liberal Christians. I mean, come *on*. The first gentile convert to Christianity is a foreigner, who is also a person of color *and* a sexual minority? If only the guy were also "differently abled" and gluten intolerant.

So, the day I saw Kelly the hermaphrodite in a Denver coffee shop, I had already written the first draft of a slightly self-congratulatory sermon on inclusion in which I took a couple potshots at Christians who aren't as "open and affirming" of the GLBTQ community as we are at House for All Sinners and Saints. We have lots of queer folk. Of course we're still 95 percent white, but that's not the point. We understand the Gospel. Others don't.

As you know, Lutherans had been fighting about the issue of human sexuality for years at this point. This whole argument my denomination was having around including "the gays" mirrored the argument forty years earlier around the ordination of women, which mirrored the argument in the early church around inclusion of gentiles. Which means that disagreements over "inclusion" happened approximately twenty minutes after Christianity started.

Much like the early church, who were convinced that gentiles could become Christians only if they changed into being Jews first (which, as we know, involved a rather unpleasant process for the fellas), a segment of the church today thinks that if we extend the roof of the tent to include the gays, then the whole thing could come crashing down around us. The tent of the church must be protected from being stretched too thin and collapsing in on itself. Some "protectors of the tent" suggest that we must "evangelize" the gays, i.e., change them into us.

Several organizations exist to help queer folks "pray away the gay"; that is to say, sexual minorities can become part of more conservative churches if they just become straight first (which, obviously, doesn't work). Meanwhile, the other side of the church, the liberal side, is all about "inclusion"; we see ourselves as the "extenders of the tent" and must stretch the tent to include the marginalized, the less fortunate, the minorities. Our job is to extend the tent until everyone fits because we believe in inclusion. And this was the point of the mediocre sermon I wrote about the Ethiopian eunuch.

And yet, there I was, now a pastor of a GLBTQ "inclusive" congregation, and I felt revulsion at seeing an intersex person. It was humbling to say the least. And it made me face, in a very real way, the limitations of inclusion. If the quality of my Christianity lies in my ability to be more inclusive than the next pastor, things get tricky because I will always, always encounter people—intersex people, Republicans, criminals, Ann Coulter, etc.—whom I don't want in the tent with me. Always. I only really want to be inclusive of some kinds of people and not of others.

After Kelly left the shop, I thought about something that happened a few weeks earlier. Stuart, the gay leader at our church who had coined "thanks, ELCA!," had shown up to liturgy wearing slacks and button-down shirt rather than his normal ironic grease monkey jacket and jeans. I like to call Stuart a "dos equis," an ex-ex-gay.

In his young adulthood, Stuart had been told by his evangelical church that in order to fit in the tent he must go through a process of becoming less gay and more straight. He loves Jesus and loves the church and so he tried. By all accounts Stuart tried really hard, and in the end it was never enough. He could never manage to be less gay and eventually he left that church.

He and his kind and creative partner, Jim, had been coming to House for All Sinners and Saints for six months when Stuart showed up in a dress shirt and tie. Earlier that day he had stood as godfather and baptismal sponsor for the child of his friends, a straight couple who have known Stuart for a number of years. After the baptism there was a little reception at this couple's house. To Stuart's surprise, during the reception, his friends rallied the attention of all of their guests so they could say a few words about why they had chosen Stuart as their child's godparent.

"We chose you, Stuart," they said, "because for most of your life you have pursued Christ and Christ's church, even though as a gay man all you've heard from the church is that 'there is no love for you here.'" It was as if his friends had said to him, "You, Stuart, convert us again and again to this faith." And when I thought of that story in the coffee shop, I began to realize that maybe the story of Philip and the Ethiopian eunuch was really about the conversion—not of the eunuch, but of Philip.

In the story, the eunuch was riding along the desert road in his chariot reading Isaiah, and he was returning from Jerusalem having gone there to worship. But I started to wonder if he was also familiar with Deuteronomy, specifically 23:1, which says, *No one whose testicles are cut off or whose penis is cut off shall be admitted to the assembly of the Lord.*" (Why John 3:16 is the most popular verse in the Bible and not Deuteronomy 23:1 is beyond me.)

This law strictly forbids a eunuch from entering the temple. Their transgression of gender binaries and inability to fit into proper categories made them profane. They did not fit in the tent. But the eunuch went to Jerusalem to worship despite the fact that in all likelihood he would be turned away by the religious establishment. The eunuch sought God despite the fact that he had heard that there was no love for him there.

So, when the Spirit guided Philip to that road in the desert, I wonder if the Spirit guided Philip to his own conversion. As he approached the chariot he may have been thinking, *OK... I'll just beat the queer with the scripture stick until he becomes what I think he should be.*

But I'm not sure it went as Philip may have expected. The only command that we know came from God in this instance was for Philip to go and join. Yet what we don't know is whether the Spirit also gave the eunuch a command. "Invite this nice Jewish boy in—a representative of those who cling to the law and reject you from God's house. Invite him to sit by you. Go... join...invite...ask questions." Perhaps Philip, in this conversation with a gender-transgressive foreigner—which consisted only of questions—learned what seeking the Lord really looked like, in a way that could only be learned from someone who did it in the face of so much opposition and rejection.

I started to think that maybe I couldn't actually understand what it meant to follow Jesus unless I, too, had a stranger show me. I regretted not meeting Kelly, not inviting her to join me at my table. I regretted not asking her questions.

This desire to learn what the faith is from those who have lived it in the face of being told they are not welcome or worthy is far more than "inclusion." Actually, *inclusion* isn't the right word at all, because it sounds like in our niceness and virtue we are allowing "them" to join "us"—like we are judging another group of people to be worthy of inclusion in a tent that we don't own. I realized in that coffee shop that I need the equivalent of the Ethiopian eunuch to show me the faith. I continually need the stranger, the foreigner, the "other" to show me water in the desert. I need to hear, "here is water in the desert, so what is to keep me, the eunuch, from being baptized?" Or me the queer or me the intersex or me the illiterate or me the neurotic or me the overeducated or me the founder of Focus on the Family.

Until I face the difficulty of that question and come up, as Philip did, with no good answer...until then, I can only look at the seemingly limited space under the tent and think either it's my job to change people so they fit or it's my job to extend the roof so that they fit. Either way, it's misguided because it's not my tent. It's God's tent. The wideness of the tent of the Lord is my concern only insofar as it points to the gracious nature of a loving God who became flesh and entered into our humanity. The wideness of the tent is my concern only insofar as it points to the great mercy and love of a God who welcomes us all as friends.

So in the story of the conversion of Philip and the eunuch is some hope for the church and maybe society itself. Under God's really big tent we can ask questions, invite those who represent the establishment to come and sit by us and read the scriptures. We all can be converted anew by the stranger, and see where there is water in the desert and enter fully into the baptism of God's mercy with foreigners, with the "not us." And then go on our way rejoicing, having converted each other again and again to this beautiful, risky, expansive life of faith.

Early on the first day of the week, while it was still dark, Mary Magdalene came to the tomb and saw that the stone had been removed from the tomb. So she ran and went to Simon Peter and the other disciple, the one whom Jesus loved, and said to them, "They have taken the Lord out of the tomb, and we do not know where they have laid him." ... But Mary stood weeping outside the tomb. As she wept, she bent over to look into the tomb; and she saw two angels in white, sitting where the body of Jesus had been lying, one at the head and the other at the feet. They said to her, "Woman, why are you weeping?" She said to them, "They have taken away my Lord, and I do not know where they have laid him." When she had said this, she turned round and saw Jesus standing there, but she did not know that it was Jesus. Jesus said to her, "Woman, why are you weeping? For whom are you looking?" Supposing him to be the gardener, she said to him, "Sir, if you have carried him away, tell me where you have laid him, and I will take him away." Jesus said to her, "Mary!" She turned and said to him in Hebrew, "Rabbouni!" (which means Teacher). Jesus said to her, "Do not hold on to me, because I have not yet ascended to the Father. But go to my brothers and say to them, 'I am ascending to my Father and your Father, to my God and your God.'" Mary Magdalene went and announced to the disciples, "I have seen the Lord"; and she told them that he had said these things to her.

"WOMAN, WHY ARE YOU WEEPING?"

CHAPTER 10

Cotton Candy

For whenever I am weak, then I am strong.
—*2 Corinthians 12:10*

The cotton candy machine barely fit in the back of my Honda, but I was determined. The young Hispanic man in his work shirt and blue Dickies closed the rear door of my car, having lifted the machine, a hundred paper cones, and a milk carton–shaped container of pink sugar into it, but not before giving me a *good luck you crazy white lady* look. My back was already bothering me so I was slightly hunched over and trying not to lift anything. The L5-S1 disc in my lower back is more like a piece of cardboard from a homeless man's street sign and less like the pillow off a fairy-tale princess's bed, as it should be, and subsequently I can't stand for long periods of time without being in pain.

I should have known better than to have stood for so long

while preaching at Matthew's nice suburban Lutheran church that morning. But when you're all robed up it just looks rude to stay seated during hymns and prayers. Regardless, after having the cotton candy machine loaded into my car, I still had to go to Costco before setting up for a special day at my own church.

It was late summer in 2009 and House for All Sinners and Saints was sputtering along, but not managing to draw more than thirty-five or forty people on a Sunday. Some weekends during the summer, when many people were traveling, there were even fewer. So, to try to get everyone who was sporadically attending over the vacation season to all attend one service, I had decided we were going to celebrate Rally Day.

A quaint tradition in Lutheran churches, Rally Day is an effort to get all the families together after the end of the summer to celebrate the beginning of a new year of Sunday school. There are often picnics and parties and dunk tanks and balloons. House for All Sinners and Saints had no children but my own and certainly had no Sunday school, but I thought, fuck it, we're having Rally Day.

It was all my idea. And like an asshole, I did all the work. That's why a cotton candy machine, six dozen burgers and buns with all the fixings, an industrial-size bag of Doritos, and a couple of cases of soda were all in my car and I could barely stand up. But it would all be worth it because we'd finally get everyone there on the same Sunday and, OK, maybe it would cost three hundred dollars, but I'd put a basket out and people would totally pitch in.

JP, one of the founding members of House for All Sinners

and Saints, came early to help set up chairs for liturgy, and after making sure he had everything he needed for the prayer station and the altar table, I went back downstairs to prep for the Rally Day party. *I hope six dozen burgers is enough,* I thought.

Having a Rally Day event, complete with a cotton candy machine at a church without children, was just the sort of random thing that started getting House for All Sinners and Saints noticed by the ELCA. That and the fact that we were almost exclusively a congregation of single, young adults: the exact population that other ELCA churches can't manage to attract at all. For these reasons, I would be getting up at four a.m. the next day to board a plane to Chicago, where I would be keynoting a Lutheran theological conference. They wanted to hear more about my church. And this Rally Day without children story would be fun to tell.

It took longer than I expected to chill the soda and stack the napkins and prepare all the burger fixings, so I didn't end up going upstairs into the sanctuary of the church until five minutes before the liturgy started. As I made my way up the hundred-year-old stairs, the familiar smell of incense and unswept floors made me smile. But the place seemed quieter than usual.

I walked into the sunlit space and took in the sight of stained glass gleaming off the twenty-six people who were here for church. Twenty-six. Twenty-fucking-six. After all my emails promoting Rally Day and the pain in my back and the time at Costco. After the great idea and the bag of Doritos and the three hundred dollars. After all of that, there were fewer people than we'd had all summer. And the whole point of my awesome Rally Day idea was to get more than just forty people at church for once. Twenty-six.

I didn't know what to do but turn around and go back downstairs with the swiftness of someone who has forgotten something and must go fetch it. But if I had forgotten something, it was my good will toward humanity.

I locked myself in the women's room and knelt on the peeling linoleum floor. *Dear God, I just hate everyone right now. If you don't remove this anger and resentment I'll never get through this liturgy. Please, please, please, I beg you. Please. Help me.*

I got through the liturgy without scowling. But only just.

The prayers of the people calmed me down. Amy asked to forgive her boss. JP asked for help with a new year of seminary. Someone else's uncle had died. A niece was born.

After the service, we fired up the grill, assembled the cotton candy machine, and placed a collection basket on top of the soda cooler. Everyone was in a good mood except me. And, turns out, six dozen burgers was plenty. The extra forty-eight burgers were cooked up, wrapped in foil, and later given to hungry people in Triangle Park. Every car that rolled up to the stop sign by the church was offered a cone of cotton candy, and some even took it. It was like the reverse of the loaves and fishes story. The tale of how Jesus fed thousands of people with a few loaves and couple of fish is told exactly six times in the Gospels, and there are only four Gospels. So in two of them, it's told twice. It might be important.

My parishioners had given away all the food left over from the dozens of people I had hoped would show but didn't, which proved to be a great joy.

For them.

I was busy doing the cleanup and resenting everyone while trying not to show it. My back felt like it might very well snap in half. I really just wanted it all to be over. I had a plane to catch in just a matter of hours. People might have been enjoying themselves, but the sooner I started the cleanup process, the sooner I could go home.

"Nadia, you're not OK, are you?" Stuart asked. No. I was a mess inside.

"My back's just really bad today," I said. True, but not the whole truth. The whole truth was that Rally Day was a failure. The reason behind having Rally Day was to get more people to church and instead we got fewer. I hated everyone for not doing what I thought they should have done based on how hard I was working. I mean, I picked up a fucking cotton candy machine and went to Costco. Shouldn't that have been enough to get people to come and put their ass in a chair for an hour?

"Jim, Amy: We are going to pray for Nadia right now," Stuart, our Minister of Fabulousness, said.

The hell you are.

But Stuart is so good and loving and not at all assholey like me. *Nadia*, I chided myself, *girl, you gotta just submit to this blessing.*

I stood there, my black clergy shirt warmed by the Colorado sun and the hands of my parishioners, and I submitted to the blessing of being prayed for. And it was hard. But then something happened. It sounds crazy, and if someone told me this story I'd assume they were lying or delusional. As Stuart's big drag queen hands lovingly rubbed my lower back and he sweetly asked God to heal me, the muscles in my back went from being a fist to an open hand. The spasms released.

I thanked them for the prayer, and they offered to help with the rest of the cleanup.

"Where does this go?" Jim asked, as he dumped the ice out of the soda cooler. He indicated with a nod of his head what he was asking about. It was the basket. A completely empty basket. Not a single dollar in it. Now I not only hated all the people who didn't show up, I also hated all the people who did. They had laughed and had a blast and ate and ate and ate and gave the food away, and not one of them put a dollar in the basket. I couldn't get out of there fast enough.

On the drive home I called my friend Sara who serves an equally odd, but much more established Episcopal church in San Francisco. I relayed every detail of the whole disappointing day and how the lazy people didn't come to Rally Day and the selfish, greedy people did and how I hated them all. And how I was a total failure as a church planter, and oh, by the way, I had to get up at four a.m. to get on a plane to Chicago; the Lutherans were flying me there because they wanted to hear about my church, but that's because they didn't get that these people are awful and I was a failure.

"Honey, just tell them the truth. It will be a gift."

Whatever.

It was almost midnight before the resentment and self-loathing shut the hell up long enough for me to fall asleep. But then at two a.m. I was startled awake with what can only be described as a bitch slap from the Holy Spirit. My eyes sprang open and out loud I said, "Oh wow." The force of the realization hit me: My back didn't hurt. It hadn't hurt after they prayed for me and it didn't hurt now as I laid in my bed, startled awake. I had received a healing. A temporary one, my back still has issues, but still...I had received a healing and I was too wrapped up in myself and my feelings and unmet expectations to even notice.

And come to think of it, I hadn't really noticed the joy people had in being together and handing out cotton candy in the street. I hadn't really noticed that some hungry people in Triangle Park got to eat iron-rich burgers for dinner that night. I hadn't really noticed that Amy, Jim, and Stuart got to have the experience of caring for their pastor and that it was a blessing to them. I had decided the event was a failure since there wasn't the right number of people and no one chipped in any money. How small.

I was reminded again of the loaves and fishes. Thousands of people were sitting around listening to Jesus when his disciples realized it was getting late and no one had ordered pizza. So there they were, faced with feeding all those people who they frankly wished would just go away, and Jesus said, "Well... what do you have?" And here's the great thing about the Gospel of Matthew's account of the feeding of the multitude: The disciples said, "Nothing."

"What do we have?" they asked. "We have nothing. Nothing but a few loaves and a couple of fish." And they said this as though it were a bad thing.

The disciples' mistake was also my mistake: They forgot that they have a God who created the universe out of "nothing," that can put flesh on dry bones "nothing," that can put life in a dusty womb "nothing." I mean, let's face it, "nothing" is God's favorite material to work with. Perhaps God looks upon that which we dismiss as nothing, insignificant, and worthless, and says "Ha! Now *that* I can do something with."

I had looked at the twenty-six people at Rally Day, and when Jesus asked, "What do you have?" I said, "Nothing."

And I had missed it all.

Hours later, I was standing in a conference center facing one hundred pastors. I clicked through my PowerPoint presentation telling stories of House for All Sinners and Saints. I told them about how we started and who the people were. I told them the fun things about us. About our annual blessing of the bicycles (a blessing of protection for all the cyclists who brave the streets of Denver) and how we once brought communion to the airport because one of our members had been denied it at her parents' church back home. I told them how we have a Reformation Day "selling of indulgences" bake sale.

I got to the end, took a deep breath, and said, "And last night I cried myself to sleep." With all the honesty I could muster, I told them the whole thing: the cotton candy, Costco, twenty-six people, praying on the linoleum, Triangle Park,

Stuart's prayer, the empty basket, my crippling resentment about unmet expectations, and the Holy Spirit's bitch slap.

Afterward, during the conference center lunch of turkey sandwiches and oily pasta salad, people at my table didn't ask me questions about how they could do HFASS-type stuff at their churches. Instead, they told their own failure stories. With heart and humor I was regaled with tales of badly handled firings and church secretaries with drinking problems and Vacation Bible School nepotism, and I realized that sometimes the best thing we can do for each other is talk honestly about being wrong.

CHAPTER 11

Pirate Christian

You have heard that it was said, "You shall love your neighbor and hate your enemy." But I say to you, "Love your enemies and pray for those who persecute you."

—*Matthew 5:43-44*

A man named Chris Rosebrough posted a photo on his Facebook wall of himself and me together. "My good friend Nadia," the caption said. He would pay for this.

Chris, under the name Pirate Christian, has a large public following as a heresy hunter. His Pirate Christian internet radio show broadcast attacks all kinds of Christians who depart even slightly from his own understanding of the faith. He is the Rush Limbaugh of the Christian world. Pirate Christian Radio says this of itself on its Web site:

PCR is an online radio station that is free from the scurvy plagues of pop-psychology, goofy fads, self-help, pietism, purpose-drivenism, the prosperity heresy, contemplative mysticism, seeker-sensitivism, liberalism, relevantism, Emergent nonsense, and the sissy girly Oprah-fied religiosity that is being passed off as "Biblical Christianity."

This station defends *the* historic Christian faith.

His "I represent the pure doctrine of the one true faith and here is why everyone but us is wrong, wrong, wrong" shtick plays to a devoted and adoring audience who may or may not be also stockpiling weapons, canned food, and Bibles in their backyard bomb shelters.

Chris is also a member of the Lutheran Church–Missouri Synod, a rather sectarian and fundamentalist part of the Lutheran family tree. We stopped engaging with each other ages ago, as if we couldn't even civilly share a Thanksgiving dinner. We'd embarrass them by inviting too many sinners over, with our trampy "all are welcome" behavior. And they'd call the doctrine police, trying to get the unsavory folks away from their table. So nowadays, a joint restraining order of sorts keeps us civil, but the LCMS really has more in common with the fundamentalist church I was raised in than it does with my own Lutheran denomination.

So after calling me his good friend on Facebook, Chris received some serious lashings from his fans, who in turn called me a dangerous apostate. How could he call a friend someone who they believed had rejected the teachings of the true Christian faith?

Seeing the shit storm on my friend Chris's Facebook page, I shot him a text saying, *Honey it's looking pretty rough out there. If you need to renounce our friendship in public I would totally understand and still be your friend in private.*

He replied, *Never. If being your friend is a sin, it's still worth it.*

But we weren't always friends....

My liberalness and femaleness and gay-lovingness made me easy plunder for the Pirate. On several occasions he had spent time on his radio show talking about "Pastrix" Nadia Bolz-Weber and all her false teachings. At first I actually liked it. I had gained a bit of national attention as a pastor by this point, and I found being noticed by people who hated my guts especially thrilling. I must really have been important, after all, if someone I'd never met would spend twenty minutes talking about me on his Internet radio show. Granted, those twenty minutes were filled with vitriol, but still...Ego and anger often compete for stage time in my head, and inevitably anger cannot be kept behind the curtain for long. No one puts Baby in the corner. So after initially being perversely pleased about being noticed, I was soon enraged for being "persecuted."

When Chris and I finally met, it was at a conference where I was speaking and where Chris had showed up hunting for heresy.

"*Good news,* Nadia. Pirate Christian is here," my friend Jay

Bakker said to me, looking like a Cheshire cat with a lip ring. Jay is the punk rock son of TV evangelists Jim and Tammy Faye Bakker. He survived his childhood of Pentecostalism and public disgrace like any reasonable person would: by drinking. But now Jay is sober and pastoring his own very liberal congregation in Brooklyn called Revolution Church. Generally speaking, Jay and I are hated by the same people.

The 23rd Psalm may say, "*You prepare a table before me in the presence of my enemies,*" but all it took was Jay announcing the presence of my enemy for anger, the heartburn of emotions, to climb up my insides, eroding the lining of my humanity. I informed Jay that I will not be talking to Pirate Christian and to not even point out to me who he is and that I hope he just goes away. Pirate Christian is my enemy. Oh, and by the way, fuck him.

The next day, after I'd given a talk about the Gospel and forgiveness and what it's like at a church where I can be unapologetically myself and expect others to do the same, several people were lined up waiting to speak to me. Standing in a large Minnesotan church hall I tried to muster up the interest and stamina it takes to greet each person with the honor he or she deserves. This always feels like a battle between my misanthropic personality (I don't actually care about you) and my values (you are a beloved child of God who deserves to be heard) and it's exhausting. Like when I have to pretend not to be annoyed by praise music, but then I pretty much need a nap.

I greeted a middle-aged lady who always wanted to go to

seminary, and for some reason she seemed to want my blessing. And then I talked with a giddy young woman who was mostly interested in all my tattoos and then a young, hair-gelled gay man who, teary eyed, said, "I wish my mom could have heard that."

That is pretty much how it goes when people talk to me after speaking events, which is why my bishop once joked about the clergy collars we wear. "You know why we wear those little white squares right here?" he asked, pointing to his throat. "We wear them so that people can project their home movies onto them."

Last in line was a guy in his mid-forties with a beer gut and a bad goatee.

"Nadia, I'm Chris. The Pirate Christian," he said. Perhaps I was expecting an eye patch or a peg leg, I'm not sure. But I was caught off guard.

God, please help me not be an asshole, is about as common a prayer as I pray in my life. And in situations like being faced with my enemy in public, what else do I have at my disposal but prayer?

Chris extended his hand to me, and after fighting the urge to just tell him to fuck off, I took it.

"It's weird, Nadia," he said. "We obviously disagree about a lot, but something tells me that out of all these liberal Christians, you and I have a couple things we might agree on."

"Great," I said, after a moment of stunned silence. "Let's... uh... let's talk about that."

And with an openness that felt like spiritual waterboarding

(Jesus holding my head under the waters of my own baptism until I cry uncle), I had a long conversation with my enemy.

Since the Pirate and I were in the middle of a fellowship hall at the conference, the crowd around us who knew about our feud perhaps expected a showdown. But instead, they saw us share a thirty-minute public dialogue about our own brokenness and need for confession and absolution, why we need the Gospel, and what happens in the Eucharist. And as he talked he cried. Twice.

I found him to be hurting and tender and really smart.

I looked him in the eye and said, "Chris, I have two things to say to you. One, you are a beautiful child of God. Two, I think that maybe you and I are desperate enough to hear the Gospel that we can even hear it from each other."

God made my enemy my friend that day. And I have not been plunder for the Pirate ever since. Chris has not spoken about me or written about me. But he does call. Sometimes we talk for an hour about theology and our families and at times we argue, but we do it with the respect of friends. We are two unlikely people who have shown each other where there is water in the desert.

When these kinds of things happen in my life, things that are so clearly filled with more beauty or redemption or reconciliation than my cranky personality and stony heart could ever manufacture on their own, I just have no other explanation than this: God.

I thought of my pirate friend a year or so later when I was struggling with writing a sermon about loving our enemies.

Some weeks are easier than others for preachers. I assume the same must be true of teachers and garbage collectors and exotic dancers. But all I know is that the week I had to preach on this text from Jesus' Sermon on the Mount: "You have heard that it was said, 'You shall love your neighbor and hate your enemy.' But I say to you, Love your enemies and pray for those who persecute you," I couldn't keep focused. I was distracted by a thought: Where exactly is the verse that says you shall love your neighbor and hate your enemies? Because I hadn't remembered reading that in the Old Testament, which is where Jesus usually gets his best material.

I called my friend Paul, an Episcopal priest from the same church in San Francisco where my friend Sara works. Paul is basically my wise, funny, gay, big brother, and I asked him where that whole hate your enemies thing is that Jesus was referring to.

"Honey, why?" he asked. "Are you looking for an exemption clause?"

Obviously.

"It's like trying to look for 'God helps those who help themselves,'" he said. "It's simply not in the Bible."

Paul was right. It's not in the Bible. But when I hung up, I realized why *"love your neighbor and hate your enemy"* sounds so familiar…I'm pretty sure it's in my heart. It's like, in my DNA.

It felt like a horror movie. "The phone call is coming from inside the house." In my heart I want to savor my resentments. Because my anger and hatred is special. It's justified.

And knowing, with as fine a point as possible, why each of my enemies (fundamentalists, Becky the bully, people who drive too damn slowly) clearly deserves to be hated can feel like a big delicious meal, until I realize I'm the main course. And because hatred is simply a corrosive form of spiritual bondage, Jesus says, "Love your enemy and pray for those who persecute you." It's one of the most annoying things Jesus suggested.

I struggled with what Jesus meant when he said to "love our enemies and pray for those who persecute us," because I don't think he meant that we should muster up warm feelings toward people who hurt us. I don't even think it's about really meaning it.

I think loving our enemies might be too central to the Gospel—too close to the heart of Jesus—for it to wait until we mean it. I don't mean it. I didn't mean it when I shook Pirate Christian's hand. And my heart, that very place where I found the impulse that I am to love my neighbor and hate my enemy, isn't going to purify itself any time soon. So if God is waiting for that same heart to feel nice, loving, warm, pink, fuzzy things about someone who is my enemy, well, I think God might be waiting a while.

So I wondered if maybe the prayer part of the "love your enemies and pray for those who persecute you" bit was about *how* we love them. Maybe my little "God, help me not be an asshole" prayer was like the smallest little opening for God to do God's thing. I don't know how prayer works, and I'm not even sure it always does, but I can't think of why else it is that I was able to talk to my enemy that day with an open heart.

In my sermon I told the story of me and Chris and how loving our enemies doesn't require the right feelings of niceness
or generosity. It requires that we commend them to the one
who has perfected the love of an enemy. It requires being in the
prayerful presence of a God who was killed by God's enemies
and then, rather than retaliation, rather than violence, rather
than an eye for an eye, Jesus said, "Forgive them." I titled the
sermon "Loving Our Enemies, Even When We Don't Mean It"
and sent it to Chris.

It was a few months later, and just two days after Osama bin
Laden was killed, that my father asked if he could read my sermon
"Loving Your Enemies, Even When You Don't Really Mean It"
to the guys at his men's prayer breakfast. Here's what you need to
know about that: My dad is still a member of a Church of Christ
congregation (although one a bit less conservative than the one
from my childhood) and the men to whom he was reading my
sermon are (to the best of my understanding) wealthy, privileged,
and both theologically and politically conservative. Later that day
when we spoke he said, "That sermon was so powerful, Nadia.
I can't imagine the teachings of Jesus being put more poignantly.
You could have heard a pin drop in that room when I read it at
the prayer breakfast." I was thrilled. Until he said, "Of course I
didn't tell them who wrote it." And then my heart sank.

I texted him: *Perhaps for those in the room who believe
that the Gospel of Jesus Christ simply cannot be preached by
a woman, it might be important to know who wrote the sermon they just heard.* He texted back *I'll fight one battle at a
time, thank you very much.*

Did that feel like shit? You bet. Did I feel betrayed? No question. But even in the midst of it, I was grateful that two days after Osama bin Laden was killed and amidst the inevitable celebration of our "victory," Jesus' message about how he calls us to love our enemies was heard. And those men may not have had ears to hear if they had known that a woman had written that sermon. This is the ambiguity of our fragile, messy human existence. I long for black and white, I really do, but that's not how I experience the world. I continue to learn, over and over again, that there are often more than just two possible labels for things.

Months later, I found myself in a situation both the Pirate Christian and my father could understand.

Sojourners magazine, which describes itself as a progressive Christian commentary on faith, politics, and culture seeking to build a movement of spirituality and social change, had refused to sell ad space to Believe Out Loud, an organization that is helping churches become fully inclusive of all people, regardless of sexual orientation or gender identity. My name is on the *Sojourners*'s "God's Politics" blog: I'm one of their writers. I also serve a church that is self-described and indeed is "queer inclusive."

But as I thought about what to say or do in response to *Sojourners*'s decision, I felt confronted by a terrible ambiguity, similar to what my dad must have felt when he excluded my name from my sermon. The ambiguity is this: *Sojourners* has, in my assessment, done more than any other organization to call evangelical Christians to the reality that a central part of following Jesus is a concern for the poor. This is a truth largely absent from much of American evangelicalism. *Sojourners* has a platform to speak about social justice to those who otherwise may not have ears to hear, and this is critical. While mainline Protestantism is on a clear trajectory toward full inclusion of our GLBTQ brothers and sisters, many evangelicals are, by and large, not there yet. So by taking a stance on GLBTQ issues, *Sojourners* may have lost its ability to be a voice for the poor in the more conservative areas of the church. Many of my progressive Christian friends and colleagues were calling for a boycott of *Sojourners* and I respected that. I just couldn't join them. Doing so would feel like limiting things to two containers and two labels, and I love that shit like cocaine, so have to steer pretty clear.

I wrote a blog post about this paradox and sent it to a young transgender man and a gay man from my congregation for approval. Having a green light from them, I posted my response.

A stream of comments that felt like bullying followed, but this time it was the liberals who attacked. They told me I was a traitor. And that it was a good thing Jesus didn't have to choose his battles. And how would I have felt if this was about black folks and not gays? I was perpetuating the alienation of GLBTQ people from the church, and shame on me.

I may have gotten an ego boost from being attacked by a conservative heresy hunter, but it felt awful to be attacked by my own people. I didn't get much work done that day as I obsessively read each comment as they came in. It was like going door to door, volunteering to get slapped.

Yet I'd started a church with eight people, four of whom were queer, I reminded myself. Our church continues to be not "inclusive" of queer folks; House for All Sinners and Saints— its origins, its leadership, and its culture—has always been partly queer itself.

"Screw them," I spit out to my unsuspecting husband who was innocently walking through the living room to go get a soda. "I have boots on the ground in this thing every day of my life. What do these more-liberal-than-thou commenters have? Opinions. Oh, you have a better opinion? OK. Oh, and fuck you."

Matthew just looked at me with that trapped "just tell me what it is you want me to say and let me go" look on his face.

Of course I knew that my anger was just masking the fact that (a) I was actually hurt, and (b) I was ashamed that blog comments could hurt me. I didn't care if the conservatives had at me. I had just never gotten it from my own kind before.

My phone buzzed and I was tempted to ignore it. But if I'm egotistical enough to read blog comments in real time what are the odds I can ignore a text?

The screen was still illuminated when I looked down. It was from Chris the Pirate Christian. *It's looking pretty rough out there for you*, the text said. *How you holding up?*

Not well! I replied, and immediately he called me.

Here's the thing: Chris doesn't agree with me or the more-liberal-than-thou group about the issues of GLBTQ inclusion in the church. But the one phone call I got in the middle of being attacked by my own tribe was from someone who is on the other side of the issue entirely. But he knew what it felt like for your own people to turn on you and he knew it felt like shit. Chris said that he loved me and would pray for me. His enemy.

Early on the first day of the week, while it was still dark, Mary Magdalene came to the tomb and saw that the stone had been removed from the tomb. So she ran and went to Simon Peter and the other disciple, the one whom Jesus loved, and said to them, "They have taken the Lord out of the tomb, and we do not know where they have laid him." ... But Mary stood weeping outside the tomb. As she wept, she bent over to look into the tomb; and she saw two angels in white, sitting where the body of Jesus had been lying, one at the head and the other at the feet. They said to her, "Woman, why are you weeping?" She said to them, "They have taken away my Lord, and I do not know where they have laid him." When she had said this, she turned round and saw Jesus standing there, but she did not know that it was Jesus. Jesus said to her, "Woman, why are you weeping? For whom are you looking?" Supposing him to be the gardener, she said to him, "Sir, if you have carried him away, tell me where you have laid him, and I will take him away." Jesus said to her, "Mary!" SHE TURNED AND SAID TO HIM IN HEBREW, "RABBOUNI!" (which means Teacher). Jesus said to her, "Do not hold on to me, because I have not yet ascended to the Father. But go to my brothers and say to them, 'I am ascending to my Father and your Father, to my God and your God.'" Mary Magdalene went and announced to the disciples, "I have seen the Lord"; and she told them that he had said these things to her.

SHE TURNED AND SAID TO HIM IN HEBREW, "RABBOUNI!"

✠ CHAPTER 12 ✠

The Haitian Stations of the Cross

I will not keep silent. I will not rest until the promises of God
are fulfilled.

—Isaiah 62:1

In January of 2012, my family spent a week touring San
Diego and enjoying a four-day cruise on a boat roughly the
size of Wichita. My kids loved the fun and freedom of a cruise,
but to me, having gluttony and frugality fighting within myself
the whole time was exhausting. I both loved the twenty-four
hour all-you-can-eat buffet and loathed all the wasted food
that resulted. In the end, gluttony won out. I rationalized it by
deciding that the more I ate, the less food was wasted, and any
time I might find a way to turn a vice into a virtue, count me
in, especially if it involves cookies or nachos.

Upon debarking in San Diego, where we'd planned to stay

another night before heading home, we wedged our overfed bodies into a hot rental car. The radio was still set to a news station. Haiti.

Shaken out of our cruise ship food coma, we listened in horror to the reports of tens of thousands dead and hundreds of thousands left without shelter, food, or family. And on top of it all, there was no running water.

Vacation over.

Pastors go from not working to working pretty quickly. All I could think was, I have to preach Sunday. I have to preach Sunday. I have to preach, and something really bad has happened and they are going to want me to say something about it. I wonder what the Gospel text assigned for this Sunday is? Matthew couldn't remember.

We pulled up to the same San Diego hotel where we'd stayed before the cruise and got the kids into their swimsuits and sent them off to play in the pool. I then sat in the lobby on the computer looking up stories about the earthquake on the Internet. The pictures of loss and devastation were rolling in. Bloggers were working overtime and news outlets could hardly keep up. I was trying to take in every last bit, perhaps so that somewhere I'd find some kind of good news to preach.

Eventually I stumbled upon a story about televangelist Pat Robertson's response to the earthquake. Robertson had crawled out from whatever kind of bottom-dwelling theological backwater hellhole he calls his ideological home to enlighten America about the reason the earthquake happened:

Haiti had made a pact with the devil and so, really, they'd brought this upon themselves.

Thank you, Pat Robertson. Once again, you have made my job easier. Anything I preach is going to be less crazy than that.

I looked out the window to see Harper and Judah, who were eleven and nine at the time, in a water fight in the pool. I realized I probably only had a few more minutes before things degenerated between them, so I pried myself away from the news site to search for what text was assigned in the lectionary for the upcoming Sunday. My hope was that whatever the text was, it would help me figure out what to say, because the reality was, I am just as baffled and faithless as anyone else when faced with unspeakable tragedy.

Assigned text: the wedding at Cana, Jesus' first miracle, turning water into wine. Great. Jesus at a big party making sure the wine flows freely. No one wants to hear that right now. Nobody wants to hear a quaint little miracle story about how generous God is when the poorest country in this hemisphere lays in even greater waste than it already did on Monday. Nobody wants to hear of an abundance of wine when people on the streets of Haiti are thirsty.

As I was reading the text, I got a call from a parishioner asking for prayer. Drew, our cantor, had a close friend, a young Lutheran seminary student, who was in Haiti building houses at the time of the quake and who died in a collapsed building. It was a preacher's nightmare—who dares speak of a celebration with ever-flowing wine when Drew is mourning his friend Ben? When thousands of mothers are mourning their children?

The events of the earthquake in Haiti brought with them a lot of questions about God, and none of them has to do with parties. One atheist blog I read that week used the earthquake to make a case against believing in God at all. The writer implied that he could not believe in a God who would inflict such suffering on so many people, which made me admit that according to that definition I must be an atheist, too, because I don't believe in that God either.

It would seem that Pat Robertson and the atheist were of one mind: God causes suffering. In Robertson's case, God causes suffering so that God might punish all the people who Robertson dislikes. In the case of the atheist, since God allowed the earthquake and all the concomitant suffering to happen, God doesn't deserve to be believed in. Either way, God is a heartless bastard standing in heaven like a maladjusted kid burning us like ants with his divine magnifying glass. I understand the impulse to see it that way. But as a preacher, I could hardly say it from the pulpit.

So during the next couple of days, I just kept reading the story of the wedding at Cana over again. I was hoping to discover something, I'm not even sure what, when suddenly, as though she had just sort of snuck into the story, I noticed Mary. Mary, the distraught mother of our Lord, might just be the key to seeing how the text spoke to our mourning and confusion.

The story of turning water into wine took place at a wedding where there was, what seems to me, a rather abrupt and somewhat awkward interaction between Jesus and his mother. They're at a wedding when Mary looks to her son and tells him that the wine has run out.

"Woman," Jesus says to his mother in a seemingly dismissive and perhaps even disrespectful tone, "my hour has not yet come."

To which Mary is like, *Oh yeah? Too bad.* OK, she didn't really say that, but she did simply turn to the servant and say, "Do whatever he tells you."

I know it's a little melodramatic in the context of wine, but in the wake of Haiti's devastation, I started to imagine Mary tugging at the shirt of Jesus and saying, *I will not keep silent. I will obey you and I will tell others to obey you but I will not keep silent. People are thirsty.* In John's Gospel, Mary is not the young virgin pondering sweet things in her heart. In John's Gospel, Mary is not surrounded by singing angels. She is never even mentioned by name. She is simply "the mother of Jesus."

So the week of the earthquake, I started to see Mary in a long line of prophets who have not kept silent. The prophet Mary stands and says, "Lord, we've run out of wine and people are thirsty."

And Jesus hears her.

Mary only shows up twice in John's Gospel, and both times her son calls her "woman." Once is here at the wedding. The other is when she stands at the foot of the cross. She watches her son and her Lord hang innocent from a cross with the weight of the world's suffering tearing at his very flesh.

So I tried, albeit clumsily, to link the wedding at Cana to the cross, since these are the only two times Mary appears. Perhaps it was a stretch. And perhaps I was trying to answer Pat Robertson and the atheist. But in a time when we were wondering where the hell God was, the only place I could find an answer from this otherwise seemingly irrelevant text was with Mary, gazing at the cross. At the cross, God enters into our human tragedy.

I've written about suffering already in this book, and I'll write about it again, because addressing pain and tragedy is one of my main responsibilities as a pastor. I'm asked to find God in suffering. And every time I go looking for God amidst sorrow, I always find Jesus at the cross. In death and resurrection.

This is our God. Not a distant judge nor a sadist, but a God who weeps. A God who suffers, not only for us, but with us. Nowhere is the presence of God amidst suffering more salient than on the cross. Therefore what can I do but confess that this is not a God who causes suffering. This is a God who bears suffering. I need to believe that God does not initiate suffering; God transforms it.

That passage in John reads like this:

Standing near the cross of Jesus were his mother, and his mother's sister, and Mary Magdalene. When Jesus saw his mother and the disciple whom he loved standing beside her, he said to his mother, "Woman, here is your son." Then he said to the disciple, "Here is your mother." After this, when Jesus knew that all was now finished, he said, "I am thirsty."

"I am thirsty," he says. "I am not watching this from a distant heaven. I too am thirsty."

I asked my congregation that Sunday if perhaps, as we heard the cry of our Haitian brothers and sisters, we could also discern other voices with them: that of Mary saying, *they are thirsty*. And that of Christ saying, "I am thirsty."

Preaching can feel like an unleashing. Once it's entered the ears of the people, there's no telling what it will create or destroy, and sometimes there's an incubation period. But despite what I may wish, sometimes (most times, really) a sermon just can't do it all.

Months earlier, my friend Sara had showed me a photo from Abu Ghraib of a naked detainee with a hood on his head, kneeling on the ground and looking like he was trying to protect both his genitals and his humanity. Sara had looked at me meaningfully and recited one of the stations. "Jesus falls for the first time," she said.

This gave me an idea. "What if, in the wake of the tragedy, we make a set of the stations of the cross out of news photos this year?" I asked our liturgy guild in a meeting a couple days before the service, when I had finally realized that I would be preaching about the cross. We were trying to plan out our liturgies for Lent, and knowing that my sermon alone wouldn't be enough to salve the wound of this tragedy, I was trying to come up with something supplemental that could be cathartic and help bring our hearts and minds back to the cross.

The stations of the cross are a traditional form of prayer in which the observer walks a path or around a room, meditating on fourteen simplified images of Jesus' suffering and death, from when he was condemned until when he was laid in the tomb.

So that Sunday, we had set out *Time, Newsweek, The Economist,* and other news sources for parishioners. And after the sermon, during open space, a time when we normally observe a ten-minute period of prayer and response, the quiet sound of magazine pages being turned was punctuated by scissors cutting thin, shiny paper. In the end, all fourteen of the stations of the cross we created for that Lent were from news photos from the earthquake in Haiti.

1. Jesus Is Condemned: A finger points to a block of darkened lines left by a quickly moving seismographic needle.

2. Jesus Carries His Cross: A man wearing a medical mask helps carry a pine box.

3. Jesus Falls For The First Time: The aerial view of an entire city block's worth of collapsed buildings.

4. Jesus Meets His Mother: An older Haitian woman in a white headscarf kneels with her arms wide, a look of grief on her face. A crowd stands behind her.

5. Simon Helps Carry the Cross: Two men carry a pine coffin.

6. Veronica Wipes Jesus' Face: A woman in a red shirt bends over to touch the head of a stunned elderly woman who is sitting.

7. Jesus Falls For The Second Time: Lying on the ground, the wounded or dead literally bleed into the street.

8. Jesus Meets The Women: With prayer beads in hand, three women embrace each other. In the foreground a woman dressed in white lifts her hand in prayer, eyes closed.

9. Jesus Falls For The Third Time: Another aerial view of another city block of completely collapsed buildings.

10. Jesus Is Stripped: A pile of nearly naked bodies in the distance.

11. Jesus Is Nailed To The Cross: A woman lies on the ground, her hands stretched out completely to her sides. Head lifted, she wails.

12. Jesus Dies: Bodies covered in homemade quilts and coats line a block, while in the distance three men carry a coffin.

13. Jesus Is Taken Down From The Cross: The body of a man is lowered from a building on a piece of steel.

14. Jesus Is Buried: A dust-covered body buried under the rubble of a collapsed building.

We choose to believe Jesus was there in Haiti. We know he was there. We hope he was there. We needed him to have been there. He was there. He was there. We will not keep silent. Pat Robertson was wrong.

CHAPTER 13

Demons and Snow Angels

Jesus, full of the Holy Spirit, returned from [his baptism in] the Jordan and was led by the Spirit in the wilderness, where for forty days he was tempted by the devil. He ate nothing at all during those days, and when they were over, he was famished. The devil said to him, "If you are the Son of God, command this stone to become a loaf of bread."

—*Luke 4:1-3*

The Sunday we helped rename Asher, he had set up a small shrine to himself as a girl: a table holding two pictures of him as a young female wearing dresses and ribbons in her long hair. Very lovingly, the name Mary Christine Callahan was inscribed across a paper scroll in front of the pictures; the flame of a single white candle caused the name to move and change hue. There was such affection in his shrine to his former girl-self.

We had come up with the idea earlier that month, when Mary had said she was going to start transitioning from female to male, from Mary to Asher.

"Honey, what can we do for you?" was about the only thing I could think to say that wouldn't be naïve or idiotic. And we decided that at Baptism of our Lord Sunday, we would include within the liturgy a naming rite. Mary would become Asher in the midst of a liturgy where Jesus was named "Son" and "Beloved."

Asher was raised in the Church of Christ like me, a fact that bonded him to me immediately, not unlike when soldiers who survived the same bloody battle meet. Asher has a strong jaw, a fierce intellect, a tortured soul, and an uncontrollable laugh. He once told me that when he started questioning his sexuality, a well-meaning but profoundly misguided Christian therapist suggested he wear a rubber band around his wrist and to snap the band every time he had homosexual thoughts. This was, of course, not a helpful suggestion.

Asher reminded me of a twenty-first-century transgender version of the apostle Paul or Martin Luther. He shared with these two shapers of Christianity a fervent desire to be good, to be "right with God." Saul of Tarsus was the most devout of Jews and a persecutor of Christians. Then, on the road to a town where he was going to go kill off a few more of Jesus' followers he saw a vision of Christ. Jesus was like, *Dude, you're killing me with this. Knock it off.* And then he went from Saul to Paul, from being the best at being a Jew to being the best at being a Christian. Only, at some point he realized that no one could really pull that off. That's when Paul finally understood grace. Paul finally understood that God's ability to name and love us is always greater than our ability to make ourselves worthy of either thing.

Similarly, fifteen-hundred-some-odd-years later, Martin Luther had a bit of a rough encounter with God—also on a road. Luther was an Augustinian monk who took being good so seriously that his father confessor worried he was going too far, which for Augustinian monks is really saying something. Luther was tortured by the possibility that even if he thought he was confessing all his sins he might forget one or maybe sin again before being able to confess again. And for this, he suffered. That is, until one day in 1517, when Luther was reading Paul's letter to the church in Rome. Luther read that we are saved by grace and not through our "works," and when he read that he realized he had been lied to. He had been told that the only way to be "right with God" was for the Roman Catholic Church to make you that way. The church told him just what he had to do: confess to a priest, do penance in the form of prayer, give money to build fancy churches, and loads of other made-up stuff. If you want to know what sparked the Protestant reformation, it was the fact that Martin Luther stopped buying lies about God and the church.

When Luther finally understood grace, there was no going back.

Five hundred years later, Mary Callahan was also tortured by wanting to be good. Based on what she had learned about an angry, vengeful God from her church, she tried to confess her sins to God, to not be queer, not be a boy, pray hard, and when needed, snap a rubber band around her wrist. As a child she would be kept awake at night with the anxiety about her own salvation: Could she ever be good enough to be loved by God? Did she do enough to be worthy of being saved? Could she maybe just try harder? She would often dream of being damned, a voice telling her she was condemned.

In college, despite her deep piety and striving, Mary would be cast out of her college ministry for being gay. Gayness broke the rules for what she had to do to get God to love her.

So a few years later, when Mary came to House for All Sinners and Saints and experienced us trying to live the truth—that God's grace is free and for all and that we are all beloved children of God and that there is nothing we can do to make God love us any more or any less—Mary, like Paul and Martin Luther before her, believed it to be true. And that changed everything. Mary thought it might finally be safe to be herself, perhaps for the first time. And being herself meant living and identifying as a man.

At the time of Asher's naming rite, I, too, was struggling with my own identity issues. I had overidentified with House for All, and my feelings of self-worth had become too heavily tied to the success or failure of the church. My ability to do my work became burdened by feelings of futility. In the shower and on walks and in my sleep I would fight very particular thoughts of discouragement. Like the torture method used on prisoners of war, the same "song" would play over and over in my head. The lyrics went something like:

Most new churches fail in the first eighteen months.
Get ready for public humiliation.
You are not cut out for this. Get ready for everyone else
to find that out.
The bishop's office doesn't have your back. Get ready to
be betrayed by bureaucrats.
You've had a good run writing sermons, but now it's
over. Get ready to fail.

None of them are snappy, but these "lyrics" got stuck in my head like a demonic pop song. And the week I had to write a sermon for Baptism of our Lord Sunday, the week Asher's name would change from Mary, I couldn't stop these same lyrics from boring into my skull like drill bits. I decided to try to shut off the evil musical theater production in my head and buckle down to write a sermon about how Jesus was named "son" and "beloved" at his baptism. But I just couldn't.

I considered that I might be fighting demons, that something outside of myself was trying to discourage me, which is embarrassing since I'm pretty sure I don't really even believe in demons. But it felt like something was trying to get me. I have very little predilection for thinking about demons or the devil or that whole "powers and principalities" thing. Like a good middle-class, mainline Protestant, I tend to arrogantly look down my theological nose at all of it as superstitious snake handling nonsense, as though it's all the embarrassing spiritual equivalent of a monster truck rally. At best I think the talk about demonic forces I hear in some parts of Christianity is no more than a result of ignorance and lack of education; at worse it's just a way to externalize our own sin. Because if the devil made me do it, then I don't have to face the reality that perhaps I made me do it. It's all so ripe for abuse, and some of my parishioners, Asher included, had fallen victim to other Christians trying to cast out the so-called demon of homosexuality, as though spiritual warfare and culture wars are one in the same. So when I felt like I might need to talk about demonic forces the Sunday of Asher's naming, it made me uncomfortable.

But I had no choice. Looking down at my tattoo of Mary Magdalene, the pastrix/patroness from whom I had received much strength and purpose and who herself was healed of demons, I knew I had to preach it. Because as I was studying the text I realized that what happens immediately after Jesus was baptized might have something important to say to Asher and me both.

> And a voice from heaven said, "This is my Son, the Beloved, with whom I am well pleased." Then Jesus was led up by the Spirit into the wilderness to be tempted by the devil. The tempter came and said to him, "If you are the Son of God, command these stones to become loaves of bread." But he answered, "It is written, 'One does not live by bread alone, but by every word that comes from the mouth of God.'"

And the Word that had most recently come from the mouth of God was, "This is my beloved in whom I am well pleased." Identity. It's always God's first move. Before we do anything wrong and before we do anything right, God has named and claimed us as God's own. But almost immediately, other things try to tell us who we are and to whom we belong: capitalism, the weight-loss industrial complex, our parents, kids at school—they all have a go at telling us who we are. But only God can do that. Everything else is temptation. Maybe demons are defined as anything other than God that tries to tell us who we are. And maybe, just moments after Jesus' baptism, when the devil says to him, "If you are the Son of God…" he does so because he knows that Jesus is vulnerable to temptation precisely to the degree that he is insecure about his identity and mistrusts his relationship with God.

So if God's first move is to give us our identity, then the devil's first move is to throw that identity into question. Identity is like the tip of a spool of thread, which when pulled, can unwind the whole thing.

For far too long, I believed that how the Church of Christ saw me, or how my family saw me, or how society saw me, was the same as how God saw me. But I began to realize something that is painfully obvious on the surface, but something that almost all of us are blind to: Our identity has nothing to do with how we are perceived by others. But it's still tempting to believe. I mean, if Jesus was vulnerable to temptation, the rest of us certainly are, whether it be temptation to self-loathing or self-aggrandizement, depression or pride, self-destruction or self-indulgence. We are tempted to doubt our innate value precisely to the degree that we are insecure about our identity from, and our relationship to, God.

So I considered all the times when I had allowed the church or a boyfriend or my own delusions to tell me who I was. And then on that Sunday, as Asher was setting up a little shrine to himself as Mary, I prepared myself to preach about demons. When the moment came, I swallowed hard and then confessed to my congregation that while I in no way have any desire to believe in spiritual warfare, that in the last couple of years I'd quietly begun to change my mind. I now think that there are indeed forces that seek to defy God in the world and in our own lives. I'm uncertain where they come from (inside of us or from outside of us), and I am uncertain what form they take (actual demons or just human darkness itself), I just can no longer pretend they are not there.

The precision with which the devil or evil or darkness (whatever you want to call it) worms into our own lives is breathtaking. It's like a tailor-made radioactive isotope calling into question our identity as children of God. And nowhere are we more prone to encroaching darkness than when we are stepping into the light: sudden discouragement in the midst of healthy decisions, a toxic thought or a particular temptation.

So, knowing these people in front of me, I made the following suggestion to my church: Take a note from Martin Luther's playbook and defiantly shout back at this darkness, "I am baptized," not I *was* but I *am* baptized. When Luther himself was holed up in a castle translating the Greek Bible into German so that for the very first time somewhat regular folks could read it for themselves, he struggled mightily with doubt and discouragement from what he understood to be the devil.

Subsequently, Luther was known to not only throw the occasional inkpot at whatever was tormenting him and causing him to doubt God's promises, but also while doing so he could be heard throughout the castle grounds shouting, "I am baptized!" This was true of Luther and it was true of Asher. And since the thing I love about baptism is that it is about God's action upon us and not our decision to "choose" God, I believe that the promises spoken over us in baptism are promises that are for all of humanity. Every person, regardless of religion, is named and claimed—baptized—by the God who created her. When I became a Lutheran, I asked Ross Merkel to baptize me, and he said that despite what I may have believed when I was twelve years old and baptized in white sandals, an act of God cannot be undone or redone.

Lutheran theologian Craig Koester says that from an earthly perspective, evil can seem so pervasive as to be unstoppable. And watching the evening news would seem to support that idea. But he says that from a heavenly perspective, evil—darkness and the devil—rages on earth not because it is so powerful, but because it is so vulnerable. Koester says that Satan desperately rages on earth because he knows he has already lost.

As I looked out into the eyes of my congregation, many looking back at me as though I had lost my last mind, I extended to them an invitation to join me in this crazy practice of picturing our discouragement and doubt as a real force that wants to defy God, then to join me in picturing evil and darkness not as powerful and unstoppable but as desperate and vulnerable.

When the forces that seek to defy God whisper *if* in our ears—if God really loved me, I wouldn't feel like this...If I really am beloved, then I should have everything I want...if I really belong to God, things in my life wouldn't suck—to remember that God has named us and claimed us as God's own. When what seems to be depression or compulsive eating or narcissism or despair or discouragement or resentment or isolation takes over, try picturing it as a vulnerable and desperate force seeking to defy God's grace and mercy in your life. And then tell it to piss off and say defiantly to it, "I am baptized" or "I am God's," because nothing else gets to tell you who you are.

During open space, I saw Asher's father weeping. I walked over and handed him a tissue. I can't say for sure why he was crying. Perhaps he was mourning the "loss" of his daughter. Surely it was a mix of many things that are known only to him. But what I hoped he heard from me was that it doesn't really matter which gender Asher identifies as. Any identity other than child of God is spiritually meaningless.

Two years later, I sat in a dive cafe eating gyros with Asher. We said goodbye as he prepared to leave for seminary. Like Saint Paul and Martin Luther before him, once Asher heard the Gospel—that Asher is loved and named by the one who created him and that this one, this God, is revealed in Jesus Christ, who became flesh and walked among us full of grace and truth and who is so for us and with us that he would go to the grave on our behalf—when Asher heard that there is nothing we can say, do, or believe that makes God's Gospel any more real, and that it is all a gift... Well, when Asher heard this Gospel, he felt that he had no other choice but to devote his life to telling others the same story in hopes that they, too, can become free.

Asher looked dapper and happy in that cafe. He wore a tweed cap, a hipster T-shirt, and a smile. He looked free. "I never told you about the dream I had the night after my naming rite," he said. "It was like so many other nights—a voice accusing me, damning me, scaring me. But this time I talked back," he said proudly. "I said, 'I am baptized, so fuck off,' and when I woke up I was giddy. I called a friend, and we went to City Park and made snow angels."

CHAPTER 14

Doormats and Wrinkled Vestments

Then Peter came and said to him, "Lord, if another member of the church sins against me, how often should I forgive? As many as seven times?" Jesus said to him, "Not seven times, but, I tell you, seventy-seven times."

—*Matthew 18:21*

holding a neighborhood interfaith 9/11 prayer service on the tenth anniversary of the terrorist attacks was a good idea, but it wasn't mine. If it had been, I might have had the foresight to be sure my robes didn't look like they'd been crumpled in the trunk of a hot car all summer. I didn't do anything but accept the invitation of the spiritual leaders who came up with the idea and made it happen. The priests, an imam, and a rabbi asked me to participate because House for All Sinners and Saints worships in an Episcopal church in the neighborhood. Just moments before the service began, I was frantically ironing my alb in the church basement. I hadn't realized how wrinkled it was until I took it out of the garment bag. Unlike the other clergy assembled upstairs greeting the worshipers, I almost never wear robes. On this day in particular, this felt unavoidably metaphorical.

The service was thoughtful, tasteful, and moving, but I mostly just stood up front with the others, a so-called spiritual leader in the community, guiding others through our remembrance and lament of the events from ten years ago. Part of the service included asking those in attendance—Christians, Muslims, and Jews—to write prayers and laments on brightly colored paper. As we filed out of the enormous Presbyterian church into the cool September sunlight, some members of my congregation were busy hanging the colored papers like makeshift prayer flags from twine strung between two oak trees. Only one caught my eye. A cheerful, yellow square on which was written: "I can't forgive this. Can you?"

I then understood immediately that my problem with that day hadn't been my wrinkled vestments or that I felt somewhat out of place wearing them in the company of other religious leaders who seemed to don them much more comfortably. The problem was that I understood the sentiment on that paper perfectly. I find forgiveness to be one of the trickier elements of the Christian faith since it can feel like forgiving something is the same as saying it's OK.

Everyone over twenty has their 9/11 story, just as their parents have their Kennedy assassination stories, and their parents have their Pearl Harbor stories. My 9/11 happened when I was a young mother and is inextricably tied to cheese enchiladas.

I first heard the news in Ed's Cantina, a Mexican restaurant in Estes Park, Colorado. I'm fairly certain I was the last person in the room to be aware of what was happening on the TV, engrossed as I was in a plate of enchiladas I didn't have to prepare or pay for. At the time, Matthew and I were raising a two-year-old and ten-month-old on his associate pastor's salary, so we jumped at his parents' offer of a free vacation in the mountains. A vacation with Tom and Lois meant doubling the adult-to-toddler ratio, and at the time, when my life felt like a several-year-long Ironman competition, adding two adults to the childcare mix was all the vacation I needed.

Lost in my plate of cheese enchiladas as I was, it took me longer than most to notice that everyone in Ed's Cantina was now quietly watching the TV above the bar. I hadn't been aware there even was a TV until that moment, but now there seemed to be nothing else in the room. There was only falling buildings and hanging questions.

Later, at the cabin, when we were finally willing to let the mundane barge into the space created by the uncertain, I sat and nursed my ten-month-old son while Grammy Lois made tea. My son's chubby hand patted my face, and I cried, wondering what world he was to live in now.

Holding the fluttering yellow square of paper in my hand ten years later, I was faced with having to preach about forgiveness to my church when the fact remained that I'm still mad as hell that my children don't get to grow up in a country where planes don't fly into towers. That is to say, I am angry that their lives might now be more like the lives of countless children in other terrorized countries.

The tenth anniversary of the September 11th attacks fell on a Sunday. In the morning we were all at the interfaith service, but in the evening, House for All Sinners and Saints had our own weekly Eucharist, and the assigned texts in the lectionary were all about forgiveness. It suggested the following texts for September 11th, 2011: A reading from Genesis where Joseph forgives his brothers who had sold him into slavery, a text from Romans that challenges passing judgment on others, and a little story from Matthew where Peter asks Jesus how many times we should forgive those who sin against us. "Seven times?" Peter asks. "Nope," Jesus says. "Seventy-seven times."

Seriously.

I thought it a bit ham-fisted of the RCL people to assign several texts on forgiveness for the week of September 11th. That is, until I realized that the lectionary was assembled in 1994. The fact that I was forced to preach on forgiveness texts on the tenth anniversary of September 11th was a coincidence. Or something. However it happened, the fact of the matter is this: Having to preach these texts made it feel like Jesus showed up ten years after the most unforgivable, murderous event of my lifetime and started blabbing about forgiveness. And this made forgiveness feel less like a concept and more like a crucible.

Jesus taught us to pray, "Forgive us our trespasses as we

forgive those who trespass against us" not forgive us but smite those bastards who hurt us.

When I was growing up, there was a house down the street that had slightly tattered window coverings, and the front lawn was like a graveyard of broken stuff. Posted on the fence was a NO TRESPASSING sign. I remember asking my mother what trespassing was so I could be certain not to do it to anyone who lived in that weird house. When she explained that it meant going into their yard uninvited, I thought, *no problem*.

Soon after that, when I first learned the Lord's Prayer, I thought it was weird that out of all the things that Jesus would suggest we ask God to forgive, it would be trespassing. I pretty much made it a policy to stay out of strange yards, and no one seemed to wander into ours uninvited, so I thought I was covered. Only later did I realize that actual trespassing was only one of countless ways to trespass against others. And now I get it—kind of. Forgive us our sins as we forgive those who sin against us. Jesus always seems to be pairing God's forgiveness of us with our forgiveness of others.

But why? Growing up, I thought it was a way of guilting us into forgiving others, like Jesus was saying, *Hey, I died for you and you can't even be nice to your little brother?* As though God can get us to do the right thing if God can just make us feel bad about how much we owe God. But that is not the God I see in Jesus Christ. That is a manipulative mother.

Forgiveness is a big deal to Jesus, and like that guy in high school with a garage band, he talks about it, like, all the time. It's embarrassing. So much talk about forgiveness can make this following Jesus thing feel like a Pansies Anonymous meeting. Slogan: Treat us like shit, we'll totally forgive you; but doesn't forgiving a sin against us, or an evil done to many, come perilously to just that? Isn't forgiving over and over just the thing that keeps battered women battered?

This is where it can suck to be a preacher. Especially when the ten-year anniversary of the September 11th attacks falls on a Sunday. I just can't preach something I don't believe. Actually, that's not true; I can preach something I hope to be true, even something I dare to be true. What I can't bear, though, is the thought of preaching something I suspect might not be true. And on Sunday, September 11, 2011, I suspected that it might not be true that we should forgive evil, because when faced with evil, Jesus wants us to be holy doormats and say it's OK. And I most certainly did not believe the other popular message preached from many an American pulpit that day: The United States has most-favored-nation status in the eyes of the Almighty, and God will vindicate the evil done to us and it is in *that* God we trust.

Somewhere along the way I was taught that evil is fought through justice and might. The way we combat evil is by making sure that people get what they have coming to them. An eye for an eye. You attack me and I'll attack you. Fair is fair. And there were times in my own life when I've been so hurt that I was sure retaliation would make me feel better. But inevitably, when I can't harm the people who harmed me, I just end up harming the people who love me. So maybe retaliation or holding on to anger about the harm done to me doesn't actually combat evil. Maybe it feeds it.

In the end, if we're not careful, we can actually absorb the worst of our enemy and on some level even become them. It would seem that when we are sinned against, when someone else does us harm, we are in some way linked to that sin, connected to that mistreatment like a chain. And our anger, fear, or resentment doesn't free us at all. It just keeps us chained.

What if forgiveness, rather than being a pansy way of saying it's OK, is actually a way of wielding bolt cutters and snapping the chain that links us? In all fairness, I should say that this is just the kind of thing that got Jesus killed. He was going around telling people they were forgiven. He went about freeing people, cutting them loose. And that kind of freedom is always threatening.

Just ask my friend Don, the Lutheran pastor who had to leave his job after doing Dylan Klebold's funeral. Dylan Klebold was one of the Columbine shooters, and Don had the gall to think that the promises given to Dylan by God at his baptism were more powerful than the acts of evil he committed. It helps me to think about Don because I realize that he wasn't saying what Dylan Klebold did was OK. He was defiantly proclaiming that evil is simply not more powerful than good, and that there really is a light that shines in the darkness and that the darkness can not, will not, shall not overcome it.

I often wonder what Don was feeling when he did that funeral. Had he so quickly moved to forgiveness or, more likely, was he just acting in accordance to what he believed? That's the life of faith, at least for me. As the great American writer Flannery O'Connor said, "Faith is what someone knows to be true, whether they believe it or not." My heart may be dark, but I choose to try to act according to what I believe, not what I feel. What happened on 9/11 was *not* OK. That's why I need to forgive. Because I can't be bound to that kind of evil. Lest it infect the evil in my own heart and metastasize it.

On Sunday, September 11, 2011, my parishioners had gathered the prayers from the interfaith service and, later that evening, strung them up in our own worship space. Our congregation added prayers and laments of their own, but I didn't read any of them. One had been quite enough.

CHAPTER 15

Ghosts in the Kingdom of Heaven

The week Amy Winehouse died, I was trying to come up with a sermon for that Sunday when my ex-boyfriend sent me a Facebook friend request. I'd not heard from Ben for about seventeen years, and when I saw a friend request from him, I mostly was shocked that he, too, was not dead.

In the spring of 1992, we had met on the third floor of York Street, the place where I had begun my recovery from alcoholism. On the second floor—the one for smokers—the walls, posters, linoleum, and even the chairs were tinged nicotine yellow, as though even the room itself had a poorly functioning liver. When I met Ben, I'd been a second-floor gal and sober for about six months. I had my own strategy for recovery: smoke a lot, eat sugar, sleep around, pray like hell, be an angry bitch, repeat. Or as I like to explain it: Be the exact same person I was before getting sober, just less fun and with more prayer. Apparently, especially important to keeping my personal recovery program going was maintaining all my old ideas about myself. The primary of which, as I mentioned earlier, was: I am an awesome tragic figure who will die young.

We sometimes make decisions in our lives based either on who we want to be or who we think we will become if we have "the thing." Cars we hope will make us look important, tattoos we hope will make us look edgy, cycling gear we hope will make us look athletic. People can be "the thing," too. On some level I chose people like I chose a hairstyle or a scarf. They became accessories, hand picked on the basis of how they complemented my ideas of myself. Apparently, the accessory my badass "look" was missing in the spring of 1992 was a boyfriend who had recently spent half-a-dozen years in San Quentin Prison for armed robbery. Which is why at that point, when I was sitting on the second floor of York Street smoking my fourth Marlboro of the morning and I saw a tall, handsome man with a shaved head and inked arms heading up to the third floor, I thought, *Might be time to quit smoking.*

At the time, I hated the idea of life without booze. But it had become clear that I was someone who "really shouldn't drink." So Ben provided me a way to still be a liquor-free alcoholic mess. With him I could have all the drama, self-loathing and badassness of my previous life (which of course wasn't as badass as I thought it was), without the indignity of throwing up through my nose.

Ben didn't know how to treat a girlfriend other than to say, "Shave your fucking legs," or to lay sweetly in my arms like a child who had his feelings hurt, there never seemed to be much in between. Which is what he was when he went to prison: a child. Now, barely an adult, he didn't know how to be a man, since he had spent the prime years of his life meant for masculine development solely protecting himself. He would insult me and then ask if I had any bread scraps so he could feed the squirrels in the park. He worried they didn't have enough food.

I cared about Ben, but I was never in love with him. I was in love with what it said about me that I had a boyfriend like Ben, and that's just different. So when, after dating for five weeks, he came to my house with a shiny handgun and asked if he could just leave it with me for a while, I hesitated before saying yes. We slept with it in under the mattress for one night, which provided me with enough discomfort to make me change my mind. At the time, I had dismissed this as a bourgeois backslide on my part, but now I know. The reason I couldn't sleep with an illegal handgun under my mattress was that I wasn't really that person. I was just wearing her clothes.

Eventually we tried living in New York City together, where he thought becoming a bartender would be a good idea for a newly sober alcoholic. He lasted about a month before moving back to Denver, where he disappeared. I only lasted in New York a few months longer than that. When I moved home, I went to York Street looking for him, and someone said he had "gone out"; Ben was drinking again. That was the last I heard of him.

So on a Monday morning, seventeen years later, it's an

understatement to say I was surprised to get a Facebook friend request from Ben. It was as if the last time I had seen him he'd been trapped inside a burning building. Finding out that he had come out alive, seventeen years later, was a happy surprise. I accepted the friend request, and within five minutes he had sent me a message saying he would be in town the next day and asking if we could meet for lunch.

I wasn't going to let my anxiety about meeting up with Ben change my plans for that day. So the next morning, like I do every Tuesday, I sat around a conference table with my husband and five other Lutheran pastors, as we discussed the lectionary text for the upcoming Sunday and hashed out what we thought might be preachable.

These colleagues don't match my outsides. No one on the street would look at me and then look at them and think, I bet those guys are good friends. And I'm fairly certain that I was the only one around the table that day who was about to go meet her ex-convict ex-boyfriend with whom she got sober when she was twenty-two. Yes, that would only be me. But it didn't matter. I love these Lutheran pastors in their khakis and button-down shirts and actually have more important things than tattoos and chemical-abuse histories in common with them.

Among the pastors who joined Matthew and me at the table that day was John Pederson, who is possibly the most well-read person I know. John's been known to show up for text study with Nietzsche in his hand, but no Bible. Justin Nickel was there, too. He is the very young, neurotic, and dangerously intelligent little brother I never had. I don't hesitate to call him one of the finest young theologians the Lutheran church has to offer. Next was Kevin Maly, a gay Lutheran pastor who is more insistent on the unyielding love and forgiveness of God than any other person I've ever met. He's also brilliant. And then there's Caitlin Trussell, who is the token noncynic of the group, and who has a hugely pastoral heart to match her big, big brain.

I reached across the table for my second cup of light-brown church coffee while John read the Gospel text. It was a string of parables from Matthew's Gospel where Jesus compares the kingdom of heaven to things like a mustard seed that someone took and sowed in his field; it is the smallest of all the seeds, but when it has grown it is the greatest of shrubs and becomes a tree. The next parable was how the kingdom of heaven is like yeast that a woman took and mixed in with three measures of flour until all of it was leavened. Then, the kingdom of heaven is like a merchant in search of fine pearls; upon finding one pearl of great value, he sold all that he had and bought it.

Silence.

After a few minutes John said, "Talking about kingdoms is weird since American democracy hates kings. So what do we make of that?"

Good point. Maybe I could preach about tyranny. Of course, I'm not sure political tyranny is a pressing issue in people's lives.

Then Kevin suggests, "Maybe the cross on the hill is the pearl in the field, and that God cheats. God cheats the system by subverting what we think is valuable."

I don't actually understand what this means but am too chicken to say so.

John Pederson seems to get it though and adds, "That's a Dickensian way to go...tell the truth, but tell it slant." I'm always amazed at the quick wit and sharp intellect around the table. I think maybe these guys actually read books while I'm watching HBO.

The conversation was great but I still had no idea what direction I'd go in with the sermon on Sunday and mostly I was distracted by the thought of seeing Ben.

Ever since I became a pastor, I spend just about every Tuesday trying to console myself when I inevitably come up with absolutely nothing to preach to my people. I figure I can always suggest twelve minutes of *lectio divina*, a spiritual practice of silently meditating on the scripture. I always keep that in my back pocket. This may just be the week I'd need to pull it out.

An hour later, I was sitting in the booth of a diner waiting for my ex-boyfriend to show up. Pete's Kitchen never closes and had on occasion been the stage on which several dramas in my life had played. Twenty-two years earlier I had sat in the corner booth of this very diner many a three in the morning, jittery from cocaine and sloppy from booze, my best friend Jimmy usually next to me. Jimmy was loud and funny, the gay brother of my first boyfriend and for years my main partner in crime. We were baby alcoholics together, and then I got sober and he didn't. Jimmy was found dead in his Reno apartment six months before this lunch with Ben, having quite literally drank himself to death. He took with him parts of my story not shared with anyone else, and I'll never get those or Jimmy back. Regrettably, I had just been too busy since his death being a Lutheran pastor, of all things, to grieve him. What they don't tell you when you get sober is that if you manage to stay that way, you will bury your friends. Not everyone gets to have a whole new shiny-but-messy life like I have, and I've never come up with a satisfying explanation for why that is.

Now I was a couple decades older, but the menu at Pete's Kitchen hadn't changed: cheap steak and eggs, foamy pancakes, many things that require ketchup. They'd replaced the vinyl and added a covered patio, which now is where folks from House for All Sinners and Saints go for pancakes after we sing vespers (evening prayer) during Lent and Advent. Usually on those nights, as I sit with my parishioners, I don't think about all the things that have happened to their pastor in that little ironic diner, but once in a while I do get slightly quiet. I don't know if they notice, which is fine.

My Diet Coke arrived at the table at the same time as Ben, snapping me out of my haze. He looked so much the same: like a younger version of Richard Gere, but with prison tattoos, including one of a teardrop, which I always thought best not to ask about. I gave him a hug that felt urgent, as if I had been waiting for him outside when he finally ran out of that burning building. I was surprised by the affection I felt.

He talked about his kids and his health problems and the fact that he didn't need to go to A.A. anymore. Oh, and he was living out of his van. This lunch ended up like several others I had had over the years with people from my past: with me feeling something like survivor's guilt. Like we were at the same place in life at one point, but now I had everything and he had nothing and I had no explanation for that whatsoever. There's just no way for me to easily trace how it is that I've gotten from there to here. Somehow I have a home and a husband, two beautiful and smart children, and a meaningful job I love; while he had three children in two different states whom he seldom saw, a bad heart, a broken back, and was living on disability.

I felt awkward and tried to avoid telling him the details of my life, partly because I was certain when he left he'd say something belittling or insulting, just like he used to, to put me in my place. But before he stood up to leave, he looked across the table at me and said, "I'm glad you're still alive, a lot of us aren't. Um…is it OK if I visit your church this Sunday?"

The rest of the week I struggled to write a sermon about the kingdom of heaven while feeling like the addict ghosts of my past were all standing drunk outside my mind's window, whining, "Why can't you just come out and play?" I just didn't care about mustard seeds and shrubs and yeast and I couldn't shut up my past long enough to write a sermon in my present. Every commentary and article I read about the parables offered me the same combination of obvious and useless: The kingdom of heaven starts out small and then gets big. So what? I couldn't imagine anyone's life was going to be changed by my preaching about how small mustard seeds are and how they then grow into big plants and that's what the kingdom of heaven is like.

By Saturday I was panicked. I thought obsessively about seeds and plants, straining for it to matter, which was especially hard since I loathe gardening. I don't even like being outside. In fact, I hate being outside so much that when I go to a restaurant with my friends and the hostess asks if we'd like to sit on the outdoor patio I shoot dirty looks at everyone until they say no, inside please. I wish Jesus had used examples taken from posting on Facebook, going to the movies, and having relationships with tattoo artists, so that the meanings behind the examples would be a little fucking clearer to me, but no. He's forever talking about seeds and vines and harvesting and plants and farmers.

Finally I wrote something down about how much my husband, Matthew, hates juniper bushes, and I described his personal battle with them. And as soon as I wrote it I knew it was crap. I took a break and got on Facebook. After liking a few posts from my friends, I saw one that said simply, *RIP Amy Winehouse.*

Damn.

Amy Winehouse, the British soul singer and celebrity train wreck, dead. Immediately I thought again of the fellow addicts and alcoholics in my life who had died while I still lived. Of course, I especially remembered PJ. I mentioned earlier that in many ways, it was because of PJ—and specifically, his death—that I ended up being a pastor. It was long before I went to seminary and got ordained, but doing PJ's funeral—as his only "religious" friend—was the first time I realized that God was calling me to be a pastor to my people.

Now, PJ was dead and I was a pastor and I had to write a sermon that mattered. I thought about how, like Winehouse, PJ was found dead in his home. I laughed out loud at how great it would have been to call PJ himself and ask what he thought I should preach about, knowing he'd say something filthy and hilarious about things that are small but get bigger, none of which I could preach about but would make me laugh. But then, it felt like PJ actually took me up on it.

I looked at the parables again: "The kingdom of heaven is like a mustard seed that when it has grown becomes the greatest of all shrubs." I wondered if maybe the size of the seed versus the size of the plant isn't the point at all. Calling something the greatest of all shrubs is like saying someone is the smartest of all the idiots. Yet Jesus says that heaven's kingdom is like shrubs and nets and yeast. It was the yeast part that made me think that PJ was telling me something. And, for just a moment, my seminary education paid off.

I remembered that yeast was considered impure (like most of PJ's thoughts, incidentally). We're not talking about the little packets of Fleischmann's you find at the supermarket; we're talking big lumps of mold, which contaminate. There is a reason why first-century Jews were required to rid their entire house of yeast before celebrating some holy days; yeast was a ritual impurity.

So then I began to consider that maybe the kingdom of heaven is found in the unclean and surprising and even the profane. At that, thoughts of my young messed-up self and lunch with my ex-convict ex-boyfriend and the death of Amy

Winehouse and Jimmy dying in his apartment stopped being a distraction and became the source of my sermon. I thought back to two days after PJ was found dead. And it became the story I told in my sermon.

PJ grew up in a nice Catholic family in a small farming town in Iowa. Not really sure how a darkly sardonic, filthy-minded comic genius came from them, but that's another story for another time. Two days after PJ's death, a group of my friends undertook what I can only describe as a mission of compassion: They entered the home of our dead friend and they cleared out all the pornography. Every *Playboy* and videotape. All of it. They wanted to spare PJ's parents any more pain than they were already dealing with.

That, I preached, is the inbreaking of the kingdom of heaven on earth. That we might clear out the pornography from our dead friends' homes before their nice, small-town parents come to settle their son's affairs. It's small, it's surprising, and it's a little profane, but it's the real thing.

I mistakenly had been thinking that the kingdom of heaven was something I should be able to find an illustration for on this side of my life. Things are better now. I'm Christian and I'm clean and sober, so surely any example I might have of the kingdom of heaven would not come from Ben or PJ or my young, messy self. Any preachable image of the kingdom would surely come from gardening and being a mom and a pastor and an upstanding citizen. But that's not what Jesus brings.

Jesus brings a kingdom ruled by the crucified one and populated by the unclean and always found in the unexpected. I'd expected to look at the past and see only mistakes that I'd moved on from, to see only damage and addiction and tragic self-delusion. But by thinking that way, I'd assumed that God was nowhere to be found back then. But that's kind of an insult to God. It's like saying, "You only exist when I recognize you." The kingdom of heaven, which Jesus talked about all the time, is, as he said, here. At hand. It's now. Wherever you are. In ways you'd never expect.

Early on the first day of the week, while it was still dark, Mary Magdalene came to the tomb and saw that the stone had been removed from the tomb. So she ran and went to Simon Peter and the other disciple, the one whom Jesus loved, and said to them, "They have taken the Lord out of the tomb, and we do not know where they have laid him." ... But Mary stood weeping outside the tomb. As she wept, she bent over to look into the tomb; and she saw two angels in white, sitting where the body of Jesus had been lying, one at the head and the other at the feet. They said to her, "Woman, why are you weeping?" She said to them, "They have taken away my Lord, and I do not know where they have laid him." When she had said this, she turned round and saw Jesus standing there, but she did not know that it was Jesus. Jesus said to her, "Woman, why are you weeping? For whom are you looking?" Supposing him to be the gardener, she said to him, "Sir, if you have carried him away, tell me where you have laid him, and I will take him away." Jesus said to her, "Mary!" She turned and said to him in Hebrew, "Rabbouni!" (which means Teacher). Jesus said to her, "Do not hold on to me, because I have not yet ascended to the Father. But go to my brothers and say to them, 'I am ascending to my Father and your Father, to my God and your God.'" Mary Magdalene went and announced to the disciples, "I have seen the Lord"; and SHE TOLD THEM THAT HE HAD SAID THESE THINGS TO HER.

SHE TOLD THEM THAT HE HAD SAID THESE THINGS TO HER

CHAPTER 16

Dirty Fingernails

Mary stood weeping outside the tomb. As she wept, she bent over to look into the tomb; and she saw two angels in white, sitting where the body of Jesus had been lying, one at the head and the other at the feet. They said to her, "Woman, why are you weeping?" She said to them, "They have taken away my Lord, and I do not know where they have laid him." When she had said this, she turned round and saw Jesus standing there, but she did not know that it was Jesus. Jesus said to her, "Woman, why are you weeping? For whom are you looking?" Supposing him to be the gardener, she said to him, "Sir, if you have carried him away, tell me where you have laid him, and I will take him away." Jesus said to her, "Mary!" She turned and said to him in Hebrew, "Rabbouni!" (which means Teacher).

—*John 20:11-16*

The first public liturgy of House for All Sinners and Saints took place in April of 2008. It was the season of Easter, and as such, the eight people who started the church together each created a station of the resurrection: a poem, piece of art, or an action that helped us experience the different biblical accounts of when Jesus' friends encountered him after he had been raised from the dead. I chose the story of Mary Magdalene at the empty tomb.

None of us knew yet how to do this kind of thing well, so it looked awkward and lumpy. About half of us bought trifold presentation boards that held text or pictures posted on colored construction paper. *"Oh my gosh, it looks like a theological science fair in here,"* Seth teased.

In the center of my middle school presentation–looking station of the resurrection I had placed an icon of Mary Magdalene, and the story of her encountering Jesus at the tomb. Below her picture was just one line from the story "And he said to her, 'Mary'"—under which people were invited to write their own names. Someone wrote "queer child." The notion that our names are spoken by Jesus, and that this is what makes us turn and recognize him, had become important to me, especially in light of how I was called by God.

Four years after that awkward Easter liturgy, our church was going strong, and for a while I had been holding office hours at the Hooked on Colfax coffeehouse on Colfax Street in Denver. Colfax was a street written of by Jack Kerouac, referred to as the boulevard of broken dreams, and known especially in the '70s and '80s as a street walked by women. When people come for meetings at the coffeehouse, I never know if they just want to chat, or if they have completely lost their faith, or if they are in a crisis of some sort, or if they are just trying to work out an idea or insight about life. What I am certain of is that there is no way to know which of these is actually true based solely on why they tell me they want to talk. One always presents as the other. I think it's the only way we know how to be vulnerable; to do it sideways.

So when Michael Meehan, a parishioner at my church, met me there one morning I wasn't totally sure what we'd really be talking about. We covered his work situation and what was going on with his brother, and then he confessed that after nine months at our church he still wasn't so sure about this Jesus thing. But he knew something real happened in church, especially in the Eucharist. "It's like that Dylan line, 'You know something is happening here, but you don't know what it is, do you Mr. Jones?'" That seemed a good enough explanation to me.

Then he said, "Jesus seems to be friends with all my friends, but the dude seems to be ignoring me. I'm trying not to take it personally."

I love it when people talk about Jesus like he's real. My friend Sara calls Jesus the Boyfriend. Once I called her to gossip how so-and-so, someone I just absolutely hated, was kind of growing on me and how I was frustrated I couldn't hate her anymore.

"Girl," Sara had said, "the Boyfriend is all up in your shit right now."

Michael seemed to be saying that the Boyfriend was not all "up in his shit," yet he was saying this even while he was claiming to not believe in "the dude," which felt a bit conflicted. To some pastors that might have seemed like a crisis, but to me, pastoring the people I do, it was almost mundane.

I didn't have any advice for Michael. I never do. I just don't have a whole lot of control over Jesus or over what people in my church believe, and, mercifully, that seems to bother me less and less. The best I could do in that moment was to assure Michael that I didn't care that he felt like Jesus was ignoring him. He looked at me like I was clearly not understanding his "Jesus isn't friending me on Facebook" story.

"Do you know the band The Hold Steady?" I asked. "They have a song with lyrics that describe this girl who crashed into the Easter Mass with her hair done up in broken glass and tells the priest, '*Father can I tell your congregation how a resurrection really feels?*' "

"Sometimes," I told him, "that's what this Jesus thing is all about." Then I offered him his own story of death and resurrection to consider.

In January of 2011 Michael Meehan, a forty-nine-year-old man, had given up. This giving up looked like him sitting alone in a cheap motel bathroom in central Oregon, razor in hand. He had bled out but hadn't managed to die, and when the police found him before the ambulance arrived, they were reportedly kind. In the hospital the ER doctor asked if he had family. "Just a brother, but we're not close," he'd said.

This not-close brother flew from Denver to Oregon, picked up Michael, and brought his broken body and spirit from near the ocean to a mile above it. There's less oxygen here in Denver, but it's still where Michael learned to breathe again after he had tried to stop altogether.

Three months later, as Michael drank coffee in his brother's kitchen, a portrait of a tough-looking, tattooed lady-priest on the cover of the *Denver Post* caught his eye, and he read the headlined story: "Guided by Resurrection, and a Dose of Insurrection; Pastor Turns Heads by Blending Tradition and Irreverence." That week, Michael heard me preach at Red Rocks.

It was a cold and damp Sunday morning. I'd spent a lot of time at Red Rocks, a natural amphitheater and outdoor concert venue. As a Colorado teenager, Red Rocks was a favorite place for me to drive up to in order to get high and look at the stars. I'd even been backstage once before, at a UB40 show in 1985. To state the obvious, I was not wearing a clergy shirt then.

It had been a long road from first sitting in a church-basement recovery meeting, to Ross Merkle's church-basement membership class, to now, about to preach to a crowd of ten thousand (or as my snarky husband would say, five thousand men plus women and children) at a Colorado amphitheater. But as I sat on a chair on the edge of the Red Rocks stage that Easter morning, all I could think about was how I was, for the second time, in the insufferable situation of sitting in full view of a large crowd of people while something embarrassing was happening on stage: Praise songs were being sung slightly off-key by suburban moms dressed in matching outfits. And since it was a worship service and I'm a clergyperson, I had to try to pretend not to be horrified.

My first experience of trying not to look horrified in front of a crowd happened just before I preached at the ELCA Eucharist in San Francisco when something mis-named "liturgical dance" was being performed. I find liturgical dance to be neither liturgical nor dance and is often performed by liberal, middle-aged women with lots of scarfy things going on.

Pretending to feel a way other than how I actually feel is not a gift God gave me. I can pull it off for short periods of time when needed, but the effort is exhausting. If something like liturgical dance or cheesy praise singing is happening on stage and thousands of people can see me, I can manage my own body language and facial expressions for a half hour or so. But then, like when I've had to be nice to more than three people in a row, I need a nap.

The plus side was that the combination of the shivering cold and the effort it took to not roll my eyes had burned off any nervous energy I might have had, so when I began to preach, I was calm.

"For many churches," I said to the crowd, "Easter is basically another word for church showoff day—a time when we spiff up the building, pull out the lilies, hire a brass quintet, and put on fabulous hats and do whatever we have to do to impress visitors. To me, it had always felt kind of like the church's version of putting out the guest towels, which makes no sense. Easter is not a story about new dresses and flowers and spiffiness. Really, it's a story about flesh and dirt and bodies and confusion, and it's about the way God never seems to adhere to our expectations of what a proper God would do (as in not get himself killed in a totally avoidable way)."

It was freezing. The crowd of ten thousand in front of me was covered in down parkas and hats, and I wore a linen alb over a cotton clergy shirt. I had to take my gloves off to turn the pages of my manuscript, which I tried unsuccessfully to do without breaking stride.

"Jesus didn't look very impressive at Easter," I said, "not in the churchy sense, and certainly not if Mary Magdalene mistook him for a gardener."

As I looked out over the shivering crowd, I suggested that perhaps Mary Magdalene thought the resurrected Christ was a gardener because Jesus still had the dirt from his own tomb under his nails. Of course, the depictions in churches of the risen Christ never show dirt under his nails; they make him look more like a wingless angel than a gardener. It's as if he needed to be cleaned up for Easter visitors so he looked more impressive and so no one would be offended by the truth. But then what we all end up with is a perverted idea of what resurrection looks like. My experience, however, is that the God of Easter is a God with dirt under his nails.

Resurrection never feels like being made clean and nice and

pious like in those Easter pictures. I would have never agreed to work for God if I had believed God was interested in trying to make me nice or even good. Instead, what I subconsciously knew, even back then, was that God was never about making me spiffy; God was about making me new.

New doesn't always look perfect. Like the Easter story itself, new is often messy. New looks like recovering alcoholics. New looks like reconciliation between family members who don't actually deserve it. New looks like every time I manage to admit I was wrong and every time I manage to not mention when I'm right. New looks like every fresh start and every act of forgiveness and every moment of letting go of what we thought we couldn't live without and then somehow living without it anyway. New is the thing we never saw coming—never even hoped for—but ends up being what we needed all along.

"It happens to all of us," I concluded that Easter Sunday morning. "God simply keeps reaching down into the dirt of humanity and resurrecting us from the graves we dig for ourselves through our violence, our lies, our selfishness, our arrogance, and our addictions. And God keeps loving us back to life over and over."

When Michael Meehan heard me preach that sermon, he was certainly not a churchgoer. He was raised Catholic but had never in his adult life felt much need for church. Yet he'd tried to end his life and had gotten it back again despite himself. So when he heard me say that God reaches into the graves we dig ourselves and loves us back to life, he knew that, in his case, this was not actually a metaphor, and the next month he showed up at House for All Sinners and Saints.

There were so many new people that first month after the *Denver Post* cover story and the Red Rocks Easter service that I barely registered seeing Michael, a nearly fifty-year-old man with a funny walk—one leg too short and a busted hip. But Catherine, a young Episcopalian architect who had been attending House for All for a while, did notice him. During the passing of the peace, a time in the liturgy when everyone shakes hands or hugs one another saying, "Peace be with you," Michael had seen Catherine hug several of her friends who sat around her. Then she came to Michael and extended her hand.

"But you are a hugger, right?" he asked and then boldly embraced her.

Later he would describe this act as entirely outside of his nature. He also would come to say that in the months before the night he had held a razor in a cheap motel bathroom that he had very systematically disentangled himself from just about everything. His business as a book designer dwindled down to just about nothing. He had no relationship, no money, and his much-beloved dog suddenly took ill and died. So Michael gave up, sold his furniture, and dissolved all connections to his own life.

"Lack of connections is death," he told me as we sat in Hooked on Colfax, nine months after he'd first visited HFASS. "The opposite of that is being able to hug a perfect stranger."

Michael found community at House for All Sinners and

Saints. He is connected there. Appreciated. Wanted. Yet while he says he loves Jesus' friends at HFASS, he has just explained to me that he feels like a stranger to Jesus himself. (Which strikes me as weirdly opposite to what Gandhi reportedly once said: "I like your Christ, I do not like your Christians," and I've tended to be with the Mahatma on that one.)

Three months after that day in the coffee shop when Michael told me he didn't feel close to Jesus, and I in turn reminded him of his own story of death and resurrection, he was again in the hospital. This time though, it was for what seemed like progressive-resurrection. Michael got a new hip.

I sat in the waterproof hospital-visitor's chair and listened to his amazement at what his life looked like now. He hadn't yet been able to build his business back up to where it was, still lived with his brother, and he wasn't yet ready to love another dog, but Michael had friends who were friends with Jesus, a place to come and pray, and a brand-new hip. And even if he doesn't feel particularly close to the dude, Michael understood death and resurrection, the basic idea of Christianity, better than most clergy I knew. And this strangely made me believe even more that this thing is real. This whole Jesus thing.

There are times when I hear my name, turn, and recognize Jesus. There are times when faith feels like a friendship with God. But there are many other times when it feels more adversarial or even vacant. Yet none of that matters in the end. How we feel about Jesus or how close we feel to God is meaningless next to how God acts upon us. How God indeed enters into our messy lives and loves us through them, whether we want God's help or not. And how, even after we've experienced some sort of resurrection, it's never perfect or impressive like an Easter bonnet, because, like Jesus, resurrected bodies are always in rough shape.

CHAPTER 17

The Wrong Kind of Different

Do not neglect to show hospitality to strangers, for by doing that some have entertained angels without knowing it.
—*Hebrews 13:1*

We have to move the church out of here," I said to my right-hand woman, Amy Clifford, as we cleaned up after liturgy. "This neighborhood is way too nice; it's attracting the wrong element."

She laughed with the kind of laugh that says, "That's funny; but you know better."

It was the summer of 2011, and three months earlier a bad thing and a couple of good things had happened that caused me to say we should move out of Park Hill, the stately, historic neighborhood in Denver where House for All Sinners and Saints had been temporarily housed. The bad thing: We had been evicted from the church building in the edgy, artsy, hipster neighborhood we had been in for three years. The good things: I had preached at Red Rocks, and the *Denver Post* cover feature about HFASS had been printed. The full-length photo of me wearing a traditional short-sleeve clergy shirt, arms tattooed and folded, and sternly looking over my glasses, made it look as though I might kick your ass if you don't listen to my sermon.

This will change everything, I'd thought. I'd imagined that the photo and the opportunity I'd been given to preach at Red Rocks would be like an "Olly, Olly in come free" for the people in Denver who belonged at House for All Sinners and Saints but had just never heard of us yet. Until that point, House for All Sinners and Saints rarely had more than forty-five people showing up on any given Sunday night (which made it all the weirder that I'd preached to so many and the *Post* ran that story), the vast majority of whom were single, young adults who lived in the city. I obviously hadn't wanted HFASS to become a sprawling operation of a megachurch featuring a Jumbotron, parking lot attendants, and drop-off dry cleaning; and there was little threat of that happening (the Rally Day experience had taught me that lesson well).

Once, in the first year, someone asked if I thought the church I was starting was going to become really big. I smiled, looked up in the sky, and said, "Yeah...um...no." When one of the main messages of the church is that Jesus bids you come and die (die to self, die to your old ideas, die to self-reliance), people don't tend to line the block for that shit. Churches that try to live into the beauty of radical hospitality and the destabilizing idea that Jesus is experienced in welcoming strangers don't tend to be described as "sprawling." *Jesus wants you to be rich and beautiful* is doing great as a message, though. There are shiny millionaire preachers and full attended–parking lots every Sunday morning in America to prove it.

Still, the problem was that the "us" could have been just a bit bigger for my taste. When I dreamed of my church growing, I dreamed of having seventy people at liturgy. Seventy people could share the work, pay the bills, and still know who each other were. With forty-five people I did more than my share of work, paid more than my share of bills, and knew I resented it.

The lack of growth in church attendance was maddening to me; as soon as we'd get a couple of new people, three would move out of town. There was a creeping futility that felt like it was hunting me down spiritually. I was convinced that there were more than forty-five people in Denver for whom this church would be the right fit. They just didn't know we were here. I tried everything I could think of to get more people. I had coffee with everybody in the city of Denver. Twice. We held quirky events in the community. I showed up to everything I could think to show up to, and yet we stalled out at forty-five, and it was torturing me.

One night in the fall of our first year, I was lying alone in bed when Matthew came in to get something from his dresser. I immediately regaled him with whatever I was obsessing on at the moment (I think it was about why so-and-so wasn't showing up to church anymore). He stood there blankly, but I was too absorbed to realize it.

Finally I groaned, "Man, I wish I could think about something besides church."

"Yeah," he responded, turning out the light, "me, too," and walked out. We had come a long way from the days in California when he was trying to convince me to come along for liturgy.

The very next week after Easter—after the *Post* and after Red Rocks—our church doubled in size. We knew that given the exposure there would be some looky-lous—people just seeing what HFASS was about, out of curiosity—but what we didn't realize was that they were going to stay, and that they wouldn't look like us. I wanted the "us" to be bigger. What I wasn't prepared for was the "us" to be different.

I knew that being on the cover of the paper was a once-in-a-lifetime opportunity for our church, but the morning of Holy Saturday, when the story came out, I and just about everyone else at HFASS had to go *find* a copy of the paper. "My people" don't read the paper. We get our news online or from NPR. Who does read the paper are fifty-year-olds from the suburbs and, aside from Michael Meehan, that's mostly who showed up. It was awful.

As the weeks progressed during the early summer, I found it increasingly more difficult to muster up a welcoming attitude toward a group of people who, unlike the rest of us, could walk into any mainline protestant church in town and see a room full of people who looked just like them. We had started HFASS out of a disdain for consumer culture in religion. Ours was not a church where you passively consume some sort of religious product produced for you based on market research. We were a DIY church; we made art and sang a cappella, most of the liturgy was lead by whoever wanted to lead it that week, and we sat in the round. So here were a bunch of people, baby boomers who wore Dockers and ate at Applebee's, who had driven in from the suburbs to consume our worship service because it was "neat" and so much cooler and more authentic than anything they could create themselves. It felt horrible and I became angry. And then I felt horrible that I had become angry.

My precious little indie boutique of a church was being treated like a 7-Eleven, and I was terrified that the edgy, marginalized people whom we had always attracted would now come and see a bunch of people who looked like their parents and think, "This isn't for me." And if that started to happen I would basically lose my shit.

If Stuart the big drag queen, Phil the aging hipster, or I walked into Middle America Presbyterian Church we might encounter a welcome that felt stretched and thin. Few of us at House for All Sinners and Saints feel comfortable in traditional, mainstream churches. But the fact of the matter was that we ourselves were now giving tight smiles to straight-laced, middle-aged men and soccer moms.

I called a meeting for the church to talk about the "sudden growth and demographic changes." I had set the meeting up with a secret plan: I figured if the people who had been around HFASS for a while simply said who they were and what the church had always been about, then the new people who really didn't belong there would self-select out, realizing it was really not meant for them. And yet even while I was arranging the details for this meeting, I knew it was wrong. Exhibit Z: It's hard to be a good pastor when you're not really that good of a Christian.

Two weeks later, the night of the meeting, it was hot and dry outside. Walking through the door of the Ogden House, where the meeting would take place, I felt the bricks of the building radiate heat like they had just been used to bake pizza. The Ogden House is a hundred-year-old, thirteen-bedroom house in Denver where young adults spend a volunteer year working at local service organizations and living in Christian community. It's an old house with no air conditioning. The executive director, three board members, and countless current and former volunteers attend House for All Sinners and Saints, and sometimes we use their front room for meetings. I set up the chairs in an awkward, lumpy circle around the room and found a place for the sugar cookies, the frosting on which had turned into a glaze in the heat.

For the two weeks prior to this meeting, I had been engaged in a heated emotional battle, but now I felt calm. I had originally been determined to preserve and protect my community from the threat of people who read the local paper and ate at Applebee's. And it had been a noble effort, but I had lost in what felt like divine defeat.

A few days before the meeting, I underwent what I can only describe as a heart transplant. The crazy Old Testament prophet Ezekiel explains it well. He wrote in Ezekiel 36:26

that God had said to him, "I will give you a new heart and put a new spirit in you; I will remove from you your heart of stone and give you a heart of flesh."

It didn't feel like a removal. Removal is far too pleasant a word. My heart was ripped out. When my own heart started to feel bitter and judgy and hard, and when I had articulated to as fine a point as possible why I was justified in such steeliness, God finally said, *enough*. And without anesthesia or a sterile environment, God reached in, ripped out my heart of stone, and replaced it (not for the first time) with a heart of flesh. You'd think that with as often as this particular procedure happens, I'd have a ziplock installed in my chest for easier access, but that's apparently not how it works.

A few days before the meeting, I had called my friend Russell who pastors a church in St. Paul with a similar story and demographic as HFASS, but with about a decade on us. I asked if they had ever experienced feeling co-opted, and described what had been going on with us.

But Russell refused to play along. "Yeah, that sucks," he said sarcastically. "You guys are really good at 'welcoming the stranger' when it's a young transgender person. But sometimes 'the stranger' looks like your mom and dad." I wanted to hold the phone out in front of me and yell, "You're supposed to be my friend!" and then hang up. But I couldn't, because in that moment I could feel actual blood and love pumping through my body for what felt like the first time in weeks. Russell was right.

I know that people who don't believe in God might scoff

at the idea that the creator of the universe has the time or inclination to try incessantly (and with not much long-term success) to change my heart. I get it. I just have no other explanation. All I know is that there have been so many times when I was so pissed off about something in my life and how it was some shithead's fault that I couldn't think or breathe correctly anymore. And when that has happened, I haven't ever been able to feel anything except so-called justified anger. Compassion is always out of the question. And no amount of self-improvement or experience as a pastor or success as a sober alcoholic seems to change that. But when God comes to me in the form of a friend who will be just enough of an asshole to tell me the truth, then it really is as if my heart had been ripped out of my chest and replaced with something warm and beating. And the whole procedure is simply too sudden and feels so literal and is too against my nature to be of my own creating.

When the meeting day finally arrived, and people started filing into the pizza oven of a front room, all I could think about was what a miracle it was that any of them came to church at all. Since the heart transplant only days before, I'd developed a curiosity about the new folks, and by the time the meeting started, I knew what needed to happen. The new folks in the Dockers needed to tell us who they were and why they were there so that the young people with the tattoos who'd been around for a while could hear what this church was really about. But first I confessed to them what my friend Russell had said to me about how sometimes the stranger looks like your mom or dad.

Michael Meehan spoke up. He told us (as he again told me in the coffee shop) that he'd had no idea what he believed, but knew that something real happens in the Eucharist. He would never have been at HFASS if he wasn't sure that broken people were welcome.

A seventy-three-year-old Episcopal deacon named Marcia said that while she knew she was a bit older than most of us, she felt that HFASS was a place where she really could pray and be herself. Next was Jennifer, a Brownie leader who had for the past few weeks been driving forty-five minutes in from the suburbs, said that she wasn't sure if she fit in this church, but she knew that it was worth the drive to feel as close to God as she did in our liturgy.

Then Asher spoke up. "As the young transgender kid who was welcomed into this community, I just want to go on the record and say that I'm really glad there are people at church now who look like my mom and dad. Because I have a relationship with them that I just can't with my own mom and dad."

Aaaaand heart transplant healed.

I really hate that Jesus' Gospel is so much about death. I hate it. I wish that Jesus' message was, *Follow me and all your dreams of cash and prizes will come true; follow me and you'll have free liposuction and winning lotto tickets for life.* But obviously he's not like that. Jesus says, "Deny yourself, take up your cross and follow me." He says, "The first shall be last and the last shall be first," and infuriating things like "if you seek to find your life you will lose it but those who lose their life will find it." And every single time I die to something—my notions of my own specialness, my plans and desires for something to be a very particular way—every single time I fight it and yet every single time I discover more life and more freedom than if I had gotten what I wanted.

✠

It goes without saying that House for All Sinners and Saints is stronger now because of those newcomers. You can look around at the 120 or so people gathered on any given Sunday and think *I am unclear what all these people have in common.* Out of one corner of your eye there's a homeless guy serving communion to a corporate lawyer and out of the other corner is a teenage girl with pink hair holding the baby of a suburban soccer mom. And there I was a year ago fearing that the weirdness of our church was going to be diluted.

CHAPTER 18

He's a Fuck-up, But He's Our Fuck-up

John the baptizer appeared in the wilderness, proclaiming a baptism of repentance for the forgiveness of sins. And people from the whole Judean countryside and all the people of Jerusalem were going out to him, and were baptized by him in the river Jordan, confessing their sins.

—*Mark 1:2-5*

Oh my gosh, we're out of bread," Rick Strandlof yelled from the kitchen, the statement putting a quick stop to the action in the church basement where moments before the commotion of Ziploc baggies, packets of mayonnaise, pumpkin pie bars, and mischievous holiday cheer had seemed unstoppable. Everyone paused but the children, who, unaware of the work stoppage, continued to slap stickers onto paper lunch sacks that read,

"It sucks you have to work on Thanksgiving. Operation: Turkey Sandwich, brought to you by House for All Sinners and Saints."

It was our third year bringing Thanksgiving lunches to unsuspecting folks all over our city who are unlucky enough to have to work on a holiday when most of us get to be with friends and family. Our "Operation: Turkey Sandwich" sack lunches mirror the traditional Thanksgiving meal: sandwiches made from freshly roasted turkey, pumpkin pie bars, and stuffing muffins (all accompanied by salt, pepper, mayonnaise and mustard packets, and a napkin). After assembling six hundred bags, we loaded them into our cars and dispersed to find any gas station cashiers, strippers, security guards, bartenders, bus drivers, or hospital janitors we could track down.

It was Rick's first OTS. He'd been looking forward to it, as the event suited his manic personality. Six months prior, Rick had come to us a homeless, bipolar, pathological liar. Now, half a year later he was *our* homeless, bipolar, pathological liar.

His puffy REI vest and Levi's had the smell of the infrequently washed and he slept in an abandoned building, but Rick is without question a helpful contributor to our church. He shows up early for every event and stays late until all the work is done. But when he offered to run out and get more bread for Operation: Turkey Sandwich, I froze. That's the thing about saying that all are welcome at your church. People take you up on it. And Rick Strandlof is a notorious con artist.

Running my thumb repeatedly over the raised numbers on the church credit card in my hand as though it might contain a message in braille for how to respond to Rick's offer, I spun around to Eileen, a nice lady in her fifties. "Eileen, you have a car. Could you run out real quick?"

When Rick had first started showing up at church, I had met him for coffee. "I know who you are," I had said at the start of our meeting, "so let's just start there."

Two years earlier, in the summer of 2009, the FBI investigated an Iraq War veteran named Rick Duncan. Duncan had been seen in TV ads endorsing political candidates and telling his story as an antiwar vet who had also been present at the Pentagon on 9/11. He had started a nonprofit fund dedicated to helping returning war veterans receive their benefits. Rick was incredibly helpful. But his name wasn't Rick Duncan. It was Rick Strandlof. And Rick Strandlof has never served in the military. He admitted all of this in an awkward interview with CNN's Anderson Cooper in July 2009.

Soon after the interview, he was charged with violating the Stolen Valor Act, a federal statute prohibiting the unauthorized wear, manufacture, or sale of any military decorations and medals. Impersonating a war vet was not enough for Rick Strandlof; he also claimed to have been awarded a Purple Heart for being wounded in action. Rick had, of course, never received the Purple Heart, but for lying about it, he did receive a great deal of time in federal custody during his trial. And a lot of negative publicity that, for a time, had his face and name (his real name) plastered on a lot of newspapers and on TV.

On July 16, 2010, a federal judge in Denver ruled the Stolen Valor Act unconstitutional because it violates free speech.
In other words, a federal court determined that when Rick
Strandlof lied about being a decorated war hero, it may have
been reprehensible, but it was legal. All charges against him
were dropped since it ends up that, unlike most con artists,
Rick never deceived others in order to steal money. He just
wanted to be liked. And he just wanted to be helpful. All the
goodwill garnered from the work he had done on behalf of
veterans was gone—replaced by vitriol for having impersonated
a soldier. A lot of people hate Rick Strandlof for lying to
them. And yet, he didn't stop.

The next summer he reappeared in Denver as Rick Gold,
convincing those around him that he was born in Tel Aviv and
had served in the Israeli army, none of which was true. Rick
is Jewish (I think). But he's never been to Israel and has never
served in the army.

Being conned is up there with throat cancer in terms of
things I want to avoid. I had already been had by a Denver
pimp and I hardly was up for repeating the experience with a
Denver con man. So when Rick Strandlof showed up at church
in August of 2011, my first instinct was to try to get rid of him.
You know, like Jesus would do.

Ugh, Jesus. He always seems to be showing up when I want
him to politely just keep out of my business. Once again, my
friend Sara is right: The Boyfriend was all up in my shit. It's
the worst.

If becoming a person of faith were more like, say, receiving a personality transplant, life would be easier. But it doesn't work like that. Over the years, most of my attempts at self-improvement have fallen sadly short. I could never manage to drink like a lady or say consistently nice things about other people or keep my car from looking like a homeless man lives in it. And that upright bass I've never played that my loving husband bought me ten Christmases ago still sits in the corner like the stringed version of an aging plus-size model. All of this is despite my resolve to change myself into a better person, a nicer, tidier, more musical person. A better person who would love Rick Strandlof without reservation.

Yet despite my own experiences of personal rejection and my years of theological education, countless prayers, an ordination, and a life centered on serving the church, I still have the same personality I was born with. I am often impatient and cranky. And my first response to almost everything is "fuck you." I don't often stay there, but I almost always start there. I'm still me. Yet the fact that I manage to now move from "fuck you" to something less hostile, and the fact that I am often able to make that move quickly, well, once again, all of it makes me believe in God. And every time, it feels like repentance.

Not the repentance of red-faced street-corner preachers waving REPENT! signs. No, that kind of repentance always sounded to me like *Stop being bad—start being good or God is going to be an angry punishing bastard to you.* This feels like more of a human threat than anything else. It never works on me. Who wants their spiritual arm twisted until they cry uncle? It's bullying. I mean, fear and threat can create change in behavior. No question about it. But it doesn't really change my thinking. Threats don't change my heart and they don't move me from "fuck you" to something less assholey in short order.

Repentance in Greek means something much closer to "thinking differently afterward" than it does "changing your cheating ways." Of course repentance *can* look like a prostitute becoming a librarian, but it can also look like a prostitute simply saying, "OK, I'm a sex worker and I don't know how to change that, but I can come here and receive bread and wine and I can hold onto the love of God without being deemed worthy of it by anyone but God."

Rick Strandlof is trying to be a real person for the first time in his life and he doesn't really know who that person is anymore. But he sees a glimpse of it at the communion table. He sees it in the eyes of the person serving him the wine and bread, saying, "Child of God, the body of Christ, given for you." That's his repentance.

And when the clerk in the adult bookstore on Colfax tears up as we hand him an OTS bag and says, "Wait. Your church brought me Thanksgiving lunch...here?" That's repentance.

Repentance, "thinking differently afterward," is what happens to me when the truth of who I am and the truth of who God is scatter the darkness of competing ideas. And these truths don't ever feel like they come from inside of me. They come in weird little packages and are delivered to our lives in unexpected ways. Left to my own devices I would never welcome the likes of Rick Strandlof into my life or my church. I hate being lied to (have I mentioned that?) and I mistakenly trust more in my ability to protect myself from others than I trust in God to change my heart. But I really do love Rick, and this is just one more thing that makes me believe in God.

Repentance is the only explanation I have for how I went from wanting to protect myself and my church by getting rid of the con artist to actually suggesting he settle into our community and stay. It was not unlike the kind of heart transplant I needed when the yuppies moved in. I was so worried about losing face like the vets and the Jews did in Denver (and hell, sometimes I still am worried about that), but the arm of God reached in anyway, ripped out my own heart, and replaced it with God's.

"How about this," I suggested to Rick the first time we met for coffee and about ten minutes after my latest spiritual heart transplant. "Hang out at House for All Sinners and Saints and just be Rick Strandlof. You're a mess, so I plan to love you, to try to keep you honest, and to keep an eye on you, but seriously, Rick," I warned, "you've got to take the edge off that crazy. Go get some help."

He agreed to this. We now call it "the Plan."

So for the first time in his adult life he is just being Rick Strandlof. But being Rick Strandlof is more painful than being Rick Duncan or Rick Gold because the real Rick has a history of childhood neglect, mental illness, and alcohol abuse.

"It hurts a little, being loved for who I really am," he told me recently. Rick has been sober now for six months, he is getting help for his manic depression, and recently moved indoors. He is also one of the loudest people I've ever met and is so spastically hyperactive that I often wonder if he's lying about taking his medication. He could be lying about everything, but that's true of everybody. All I know for sure is that he's still unbelievably helpful at every church function and that he is loved and wanted at House for All.

In the fall of 2011, during the Occupy Denver actions, he organized and oversaw all of the food distribution at the hub of the local protests. "Distributing food at Occupy Denver is awesome!" Rick chirped to me over the phone. "Everyone is fed. It's doesn't matter if you are a homeless guy who is scamming and doesn't even care about Occupy or a lawyer on a lunch break." He pauses. "The only place I've ever really seen that is at communion." As we hung up, I tried to pretend that I wasn't crying.

CHAPTER 19

Beer & Hymns

We weren't really able to sing over the sounds of the crowded Irish pub that night, but we sang within it, through it, like a sacred countermelody to chaos. House for All's quarterly Beer & Hymns (or in Rick Strandlof's and my case, Diet Coke & Hymns) event had ended moments earlier but, oddly, rather than going home, we began to sing evening prayers, called vespers. Singing vespers in a bar is something even *we* had never done, but it was July 20, 2012, and nineteen hours earlier and nine miles east of us, a gunman had walked into a midnight showing of a Batman movie and opened fire, killing twelve people and injuring dozens more. Some of our friends had been in that theater. Not shot, but injured all the same, in ways no one who had not been there would ever fully realize.

Beer & Hymns takes place every few months; we generally cram as many people as we can into the basement of a bar and belt out old hymns, pint glasses raised high, and for months it had been scheduled for that night. For a moment, after the shooting, I had considered canceling it. But that idea passed quickly. Instead I posted on Facebook that that night we would still gather to sing praises to God, for, as the funeral mass says, "even as we go to the grave still we make our song alleluia."

Besides, people need to be together when tragedy happens. We may not know what to say or what to do, but we just have to share space with other people. And if we are going to share space together in public, hours after a massacre happened just a few miles away, then what better thing can we do than sing hymns to God? So rather than cancel Beer & Hymns we occupied it. There was an appropriately less-raucous feeling to the event than normal, but there was something new in the air, too. I saw it in the determined way that Jim and Stuart and Amy were lifting their pint glasses as we sang: "It is well, it is well with my soul."

It took a few minutes for me to pinpoint the uniqueness of how these hymns were being sung. But then I knew. It was defiance.

Two days later, we gathered for our weekly Eucharist on Sunday, July 22, which happens to be the Feast Day of Saint Mary Magdalene, my patroness. Again, I considered canceling our celebration of this saint, going instead with the regularly assigned readings for the day. But then I reread the resurrection account from John 20, and I knew that Mary Magdalene could help me preach about death and resurrection, just as she had countless times before.

My former bishop Allan Bjornberg once said that the greatest spiritual practice isn't yoga or praying the hours or living in intentional poverty, although these are all beautiful in their own way. The greatest spiritual practice is just showing up. And Mary Magdalene is the patron saint of just showing up. Showing up, to me, means being present to what is real, what is actually happening. Mary Magdalene didn't necessarily know what to say or what to do or even what to think when she encountered the risen Jesus. But none of that was nearly as important as the fact that she was present and attentive to him.

Seven years ago, I got a tattoo of Mary Magdalene on my forearm when I realized that I, as unlikely a woman as any, was called to be a preacher of the Gospel. Beginning when I first told my parents about my calling, the tattoo has often made me feel empowered to borrow Mary's voice and her ability to show up. Mary was the very first to proclaim, in the midst of loss and sorrow, that death had been defeated. And on that Friday of the shooting, I needed her badly. Mary would not have shied away from naming the darkness and despair of an event like the movie theater massacre. She was familiar with darkness, after all.

Luke tells us that it was from Mary Magdalene that

Jesus cast out seven demons. Then, having been freed from her demons, she followed Jesus and, as the text tells us, she supported the ministry from her own pocketbook. In the end it was Mary Magdalene who did not deny Jesus, nor betray Jesus, nor hightail it out when things got rough, but with just a couple of other faithful women, she stood at the cross. And after Jesus died, it was Mary who came to his tomb while it was still dark. She stood there and wept. She did not recognize the resurrected Christ until he spoke her name, but she turned at the sound of it. And it was her, a deeply faithful and deeply flawed woman, whom Jesus chose to be the first witness of his resurrection and to whom he commanded to go and tell every-one else about it.

If Saint Mary Magdalene had been the "pastrix" of my congregation, she would not have shied away from the news of innocent people slaughtered while it was still dark. She would have showed up and named the event from two days prior exactly what it was: horrific, evil, senseless violence without a shred of anything redemptive about it. And that was what I had decided to do.

Of course, Mary Magdalene would have very little toler-ance for the Christian platitudes and vapid optimism that seem to swirl around these kinds of tragic events. Those plati-tudes are tempting, but they're nothing but luxuries for peo-ple who've never had demons (or at least have never admitted to them). But equally, she would reject nihilism, or the idea that there is no real meaning in life or death—ideas present in so much of postmodernity. Those ideas, too, are luxuries, but they are for those who have never been freed from demons.

What Mary *would* do is show up and remind us that despite the violence and fear, it's still always worth it to love God and to love people. And always, always, it is worth it to sing alleluia in defiance of the devil, who surely hates the sound of it.

On the Sunday after the massacre, I stood before our congregation, grasping the music stand, which holds my sermon notes, and I looked at my now slightly faded tattoo of Mary Magdalene. In the image, she stands tall with one hand in a gesture of openness and the other with a raised finger as if to say, *Shut up, because I have to tell you something.* For not the first time nor the last, I borrowed her voice.

I preached about how two nights earlier, when we sang hymns to God at the bar, it had sounded like a people who simply would not believe that violence wins, a people who know that the sound of the risen Christ speaking our names drowns out all other voices. It drowns out the sound of the political posturing, the sound of cries for vengeance, the sound of our own fears and anxieties, *and* the deafening uncertainty—because all of it is no match for the shimmering sound of the resurrected Christ calling our name.

This is the resurrected God to whom we sing. A God who didn't say we would never be afraid but that we would never be alone. Because this is a God who shows up: in the violence of the cross, in the darkness of a garden before dawn, in the gardener, in a movie theater, in the basement of a bar.

And then, in the middle of my sermon, surprising even myself, I did not speak the Trisagion, which is from the Good Friday liturgy: "Holy God, Holy and Mighty, Holy and Immortal have mercy upon us." This time, I sang it. My voice was not totally certain when out of it came, "Holy God," but as I sang the familiar chant from Good Friday, others joined in, "Holy and Mighty." And by the time I sang, "Holy and Immortal," half of the room was singing with me, which was a blessing, since my voice cracked with emotion through "Have mercy upon us." And after the service, during open space, I wept.

Singing in the midst of evil is what it means to be disciples. Like Mary Magdalene, the reason we can stand and weep and listen for Jesus is because we, like Mary, are bearers of resurrection, we are made new. On the third day, Jesus rose again, and we do not need to be afraid. To sing to God amidst sorrow is to defiantly proclaim, like Mary Magdalene did to the apostles, and like my friend Don did at Dylan Klebold's funeral, that death is not the final word. To defiantly say, once again, that a light shines in the darkness and the darkness cannot, will not, shall not overcome it. And so, evil be damned, because even as we go to the grave, still we make our song alleluia. Alleluia. Alleluia.

Moments later, as I served my parishioners the Eucharist, I looked each person in the eye and said, "Child of God, the body of Christ, broken for you."

After the service, I stood at the door of the church, where I station myself each week after liturgy so I can catch people when they leave. The hand of a visitor reached out to mine and then turned my wrist.

"So that's Mary Magdalene?" the wrist turner asked, as she took in the tattoo that covers my right forearm, elbow to wrist.

"Yep," I told the visitor, trying to not appear annoyed at being touched by a stranger.

"Why did you choose her?" she asked, with a slightly disapproving tone (although I could have just imagined that part).

"I guess so I could remind myself that I have the authority to do this," I gestured to the mob of people, my people, milling about. They were laughing, finishing off the bread and wine from communion, passing around a new baby; others were stacking chairs, some with the slight annoyance of people working while everyone else is milling/laughing/baby passing.

I saw John and Maria, a quirky hipster couple, holding hands; they met at HFASS, and a year earlier I'd performed their wedding and now it was their new baby being passed around. I saw Aaron the tall, geeky engineer laughing with Jamie the cantor. I saw Rick Strandlof putting away chairs and making everyone laugh. I saw Krista the six-foot-tall, red-headed daughter of a Lutheran bishop embracing Stuart the drag queen, and it dawned on me then that none of these people would have known each other were it not for the church I started out of my living room and my own desire to be a part of a community.

The day before, I baked the communion bread. Adding the molasses is always the best part. It turns everything caramely brown, and I watched as the stickiness of it was lost in the dough. Twenty minutes later my kids and I tore into the extra loaf, popping bites into our mouths before the butter we slathered on it had a chance to melt fully. It was chewy and filling and not even a little bit dry and sandy, as the bread I had once tried baking at the Humboldt House. Lots of things had changed since then, the least of which was my inability to bake bread.

This is my spiritual community, where messy, beautiful people come as they are to gather around a story and a table—where truth and molassesy bread are shared—and it is simply the thing I was meant to do.

Once, a seminary student asked to shadow me for two days to see what my life as a pastor was like. At the end, he said, "Oh my gosh, you're basically *a person* for a living." I get to be a person for a living. A person who every morning thinks about her quirky little church and prays, *Oh God, it's so beautiful. Help me not fuck it up.*

The visitor at the door of the church had moved on to my other tattoos: Lazarus raised from the grave and, on the other arm, images of the liturgical year. And for a moment I was back in my parents' living room almost seven years earlier, trying not to scratch at the brand-new tattoo of Mary Magdalene as I nervously told them I was going to be a Lutheran pastor.

Without realizing it, I was scratching again at the now less vibrant tattoo of Mary Magdalene, and the church visitor asked if it still itched.

"Uh, only spiritually," I answered, not even really sure what that meant. But I kept scratching, while the alleluias rang through my head.

Acknowledgments

To Greg Campbell. I didn't manage to make you a Lutheran. But you may have managed to make me a writer.

To my agent Greg Daniel who gets me and fights for me and sometimes even tells me what I need (but do not want) to hear.

To Nicci Jordan Hubert who I'm pretty sure God sent to be my editor.

To my "little brother" Justin Nickel who makes me feel smarter just by being around him and who has given me some of the confidence needed to write this book.

To my friends and fellow writers Sara Miles, Paul Fromberg, Tony Jones, Doug Pagitt, Rachel Held Evans, Lauren Winner, Enuma Okoro, Kae Evenson, Rachel Swan, Melissa Febos, Shane Hipps, Frank Schaeffer, Brian McLaren, and Phyllis Tickle who pick up the phone when I call. Please don't ever let other people know how needy I can be.

To my pastoral colleagues John Pederson, Caitlin Trussell, Jim Gonia, Kevin Maly, Jodi Hogue, Jodi-Renee Adams, Ruth Woodliff-Stanley, Jerry Herships, and Heather Haginduff who always show me Jesus.

To Jane Vennard for her wise direction.

To Courtney Perry for the amazing photos.

To Wendy and all the great folks at Jericho for risking so much by believing in me and in this book.

To Pomegranate Place, the Lighthouse Writers Workshop, and Jenny Morgan & Kristy Jordon for spaces to write.

To my extended family Barbara & David Lehr, Gary & Elizabeth Bolz, and Tom & Lois Weber for your kindness and support, and to my husband Matthew, daughter Harper and son Judah for loving me even though you really know me.

To the beautiful and broken people of House for all Sinners and Saints—thank you for letting me be your pastor and allowing me to tell your stories. It is an honor and a privilege. You make me want to be Christian and that's saying a lot.